MY EYES ONLY LOOK OUT

D0544611

For two very special people:
my daughter, Mia,
and my mother, Annie

Margaret McCarthy

MY EYES ONLY
LOOK OUT

BRANDON

Brandon Original Paperback

This edition published in 2001 by
Brandon
an imprint of Mount Eagle Publications

10 9 8 7 6 5 4 3 2 1

Copyright © Margaret McCarthy 2001

The author has asserted her moral rights.

British Library Cataloguing in Publication Data is available for this book.

ISBN 0 86322 284 6
(original paperback)

Cover design by id communications, Tralee
Typeset by Red Barn Publishing, Skibbereen
Printed by The Guernsey Press Ltd, Channel Islands

Contents

Acknowledgements

Many people contributed to bringing this book to life. The National Committee for Development Education provided me with a research grant in 1995 which generated the idea for the book. Various people helped in practical ways: Noel O'Reilly and Rose McAllorum, Rose Brock, Marie Power, Cathal Dervan, Adekunle Gomez, my brother Michael McCarthy and Emeli Ó hAilpín. Angela Marini of Marini Creative Photography provided some of the photographs for this book, and thanks also to Aoife of Sportsfile Photographic Agency. For their help and encouragement I would like to thank Paul Cullen, Abel Ugba and Caroline Wilson, as well as Liam O'Meara and Michael O'Flanagan. My grateful thanks to Marian Tannam and also to Anne McDonnell. My daughter, Mia, urged me forward, and Emmanuel contributed his part in the journey. I am grateful to all at Brandon. The essence of this work is the contributors. Words are not adequate to describe what a pleasure it was to be involved with them in this book. They are courageous, honest, generous and beautiful, and I thank them all.

Publisher's note

Some of the people interviewed for this book have chosen not to have photographs of them included, and some have chosen not to have their real names used; all have approved the publication of their interviews.

Introduction

In the autumn of 1978, finding myself young and pregnant and having discarded the idea of abortion, I moved on to that of adoption. I was slightly familiar with the term "unmarried mother", but I didn't personally know any at that time. Birth outside of marriage was still shameful and unacceptable, certainly where I came from. Through whispered comments and sad head shakes, I had learnt that several sisters in a neighbouring family had become pregnant and had been banished to the Good Shepherd's Home in Cork. Their babies were taken and, I suppose, put up for adoption, and these women stayed on in the convent, their days busy with menial labour while they served out their earthly penance. Every few years, they would be let out to visit their remaining relatives in the family home. These were nondescript, homely women in late middle age who favoured floral aprons and slippers. To my mind, they were the most inoffensive and certainly the most asexual people you could meet. To the observer, they bore no sign of their youthful transgressions, yet they were to pay for them with their lives and their loss of liberty. Even then I felt there was barbarism at work, a cruel and extreme punishment that the rest of the community appeared to be comfortable with. And because my world was fairly narrow, these women were my only role models of single parenthood, although the year was 1978.

Not surprising, therefore, that I thought adoption would be an option for myself and the baby, due in June of 1979. I had loved Emmanuel, the baby's father, very deeply, but the nonchalance covering the awkwardness of my youth meant that I had not made plans about the future. Our paths were diverging. My insecurity led me to plan instead for contingencies and so avoid the possibility of rejection, and this was why on a soft, spring day I was keeping an appointment with the social worker in the adoption agency. In the course of the visit, I asked a question that had been on my mind from the beginning and one to which I already knew the answer. The woman confirmed that, as the baby's father was black, it would be more difficult to find a family. But never mind, she added bravely, there were more families than babies available so a family would be found. Second-class baby. The implications remained unsaid. That notion did not correspond with my idea of what this baby would be like. At a most basic level, it didn't make any sense to me that here I was trying to secure the best future for this child while at the same time being made aware that it was being labelled even before being born as being disadvantaged. At the end of the day, it seemed repugnant. I felt that both Emmanuel and I were reasonably intelligent and healthy people and that, as I had already started studying for a degree, I should be able to provide a home for a child, even though it would be as a single parent. It was my outrage at the assumption of colour resulting in a flawed child that allowed me to overcome my tremendous fears and insecurities and cowardice and my desire to turn the clock back and not be pregnant.

In 1981, as Mia approached her third birthday, I took her on a trip to Southern Africa. I was to take part in voluntary work in a rural part of Lesotho, and I also thought it would be an opportunity to introduce her to her father, who by then had returned to Zimbabwe. It was necessary for us to travel through Botswana and South Africa. We had all heard about apartheid, and South Africa was disbarred from membership of most groupings of civilised nations due to maintaining a system where the black majority were disenfranchised and discriminated against. I was determined to keep a low profile and not linger in South Africa. Even at that, I was accosted twice by South African men, once in Harare and once in Johannesburg; they fitted into a certain Afrikaner stereotype — thickset and overweight. I can't remember their exact words to me, but the gist of what they said to me was, how could I lower myself to give birth to something like *that*? — indicating my daughter. And I remember feeling no hurt or upset at the time, as their insults just confirmed my feelings that they were part of an inhuman and backward system that was unique in the modern world. Strange then that today in Ireland I hear people making similar remarks to people perceived as immigrants with darker skins. It is shocking to realise that they must feel immune to censure from the general population.

1995. Darkness falls early and the nights draw in with the inevitable turn towards autumn as a young girl stands at Aston Quay in Dublin, waiting for a bus to take her home. Being Sunday, the city is not as full as usual with night-time revellers. Suddenly she hears shouts of "Niggers out. Keep Ireland white." Approaching the bus stop, she sees the figure of a man dressed from head to toe in black and topped off with a balaclava. He is closely followed by about seven similarly dressed individuals, some without balaclavas; they are a mixture of men and women in their twenties. Walking slightly ahead, the man in the balaclava appears to be their leader. All are chanting the same racist slogans in unison and saluting in Nazi style with military precision. As he passes, he is so close to her that she can hear his breathing through the roughly cut gap in his balaclava. She presses herself into the recess of the doorway, hoping, praying that this sinister convoy will pass by without noticing her. They continue down the street and turn the corner towards Temple Bar — Dublin's "Left Bank" area. There is a scattering of people at the bus stop. Nobody seems to think much of this strange convoy, or if they do they are keeping it to themselves.

This young girl was my daughter. When I heard this story, I was both sad and angry. I was sad because when children are young they get a lot of positive attention, and when they are adolescent and pretty like my daughter and in a minority, they are seen as a novelty. I am not attempting to be "colour blind", but I still believe that your life and your personality should not be dictated by the tone of your skin colour. I believe that people are complex beings and a multitude of differences are at work in every one of us.

Ever since the birth of my daughter, Mia, I have always wondered how it was for other people of mixed-race parentage growing up in this country. This is a collection of other people's stories, people with one black and one white parent — people like my daughter. It gives a snapshot of what it was like for them. Most are in their thirties, but a small number are younger, and it is interesting to contrast the differences of their experiences.

So, at the start of this new Millennium, it is not easy for a non-white person living in Ireland. It is difficult to predict the future beyond speculation and careful optimism. Some things are different today. Others are not. Questions like "Where do you come from?" and assumptions like "I bet you like the hot weather" are a sometimes amusing, other times tiresome reminder of difference. The situation in Ireland is unusual in that it remains a more or less monocultural society despite the disproportionate amount of attention that has been focused on the arrival of asylum seekers and other immigrants to this country.

There is no doubt that racism hurts all of us and holds us back as a people. We are faced with no choice but to work against racism wherever it manifests itself so as to make this a better place to live for everyone. It will take some time before people will relate to the individual before their colour, but hopefully that day will also come.

When asked to comment on things they liked about themselves, the people interviewed for this book tended to mention positive attributes like physical attractiveness and good physique, but it could be said in their case their beauty is more than skin deep as they bare their souls and their hearts and share parts of themselves.

Margaret McCarthy

Caroline

THE LITTLE BLACK BABY

Separated from her husband, Caroline lives with her children in a sprawling west Dublin housing estate.

Her earliest memories are of life in a special school where she stayed until she was fourteen years old. Later she found she was one of eight children; the only child who was of mixed-race appearance, she was the only one to have been placed in care.

Prior to this interview, although Caroline had traced her history from infancy, she had not yet come to terms with it.

Early memories

I was born in the Coombe Hospital in Dublin. My earliest memories are from about the age of four. All the memories of childhood would have been of school, although I didn't remember how I got to the school or anything like that. It was a boarding school called Glenmaroon and was run by nuns of the Holy Angels in Chapelizod at the side of Phoenix Park.

The nuns used to tell me that I had no parents. I remember, when I was really young, one nun saying to me, "You have no mammy or daddy," but it wasn't as though she was being bad to me or anything like that. When I was young, nobody in the school mentioned parents, and I didn't know what they really were, although this changed as I got older. Some girls used to go home at weekends, and I became aware of them being gone and that we had to stay. At times I'd get sad thinking about it because I would realise that there was more to it than living in the school all the time. Sometimes, on Sundays or when the school plays were on, a few parents used to come to see

13

their children, and I would always dream that mine would come some day, but it never happened.

If you did something wrong, the nuns would always say, "I'll ring your parents." Sometimes I would deliberately do something wrong, but, although I'd be punished, they never sent for my parents. I always thought that my parents were African. Then, one day when I was fourteen, my mother came to the school. We were supposed to be gone swimming, but I had been sent to bed as a punishment. It was a great shock when I was told I was going to meet my mother as I hadn't realised that I had a family. My brother, who was a bit older than me, came with her. My mother sat at one end of this big table: I stayed at my end of the table and she stayed at her end. She looked nice, real dark hair. She didn't look like my mother though. She only stayed a few minutes and then she left.

The school

Most of the girls in the school had a mental handicap. Some would have a physical handicap, but not that many. Myself and others who would be classed as "normal" knew that they were slower than us by the way that they behaved and the things that they did. But we were all put in the same room and did the same lessons, so you wouldn't expand your brain, and there was no encouragement to do better. Well, I suppose there were loads of activities, but academically, it was basic. For example, I have always had a hang-up about maths. I have come on a lot, but I feel if I had gone to an ordinary school, I don't think I would have had as much trouble as I went through life. There are many things I am grateful for; I am an avid reader, and it is thanks to the school that I got some education. I can read and write, and that is a lot.

The classes were up to twelve, but it was specifically for children who were mildly mentally handicapped, and the lessons were geared like that. If they decided a child was there because she had no parents but intellectually she was OK, then she went out to school in Ballyfermot.

A few of the girls I knew went out to school. One even went to a college. Unfortunately, today, she is not doing too well either, but her background is like mine. She was given away, too. She would have done well — academically, she has the brains — but it is just her background. There was nobody to support her, and that was where she fell down.

Most of the nuns were very good. One nun I was really close to. We used to talk about everything. I used to fill her hot water bottle for her, and sometimes she would fill mine. I used to say to her, "I wish you were my mum." She was really nice. She could be quite cross as well, but having said that, we still got on. I still go back to visit.

I blame my parents for a lot of things. You see, I think if my parents didn't want me, I would have preferred if they had given me up for adoption. I feel many of the things that I can't do today arise from the fact that I went to a special school. I am very shy and inhibited. In ways, I seem to be my own worst enemy, because I have no ambition or drive. I am too shy to be outspoken or to do the things I would really like to do. Also, I feel nobody will expect me to do these things because I was in a special school, and I find myself using that as an excuse.

Leaving school and afterwards

I had seen some of my friends leave before me. Some of them, their parents came up to Dublin to take them home; but other girls, like me, who didn't have a family to go to, they went on to the hostel. When it came to my turn to leave, I didn't want to, especially because of the nun whom I was very close to. I didn't know what it was going to be like. I mean, I used to go into town, but it would always be with a teacher and as a group. I had stayed longer than I should have because I didn't have a job. Then the nuns got me a job in Boylan's café. I used to travel in and out, but it was time to leave school. I cried the day I was leaving.

I was sixteen when I went to the hostel. It was a small house owned by the nuns on the North Circular Road. At sixteen I was very immature, very young. I didn't know anything about life or about what happened when you left school. I didn't know what to do with my time. I have always found it very difficult to make friends and to join in activities with other people. I wanted to make a new life, but then I realised the only girls I knew were in the hostel. Really, I had no friends, and the girls in the hostel were in the same situation as me, because they wanted to break out and make friends, but they didn't know how to go about it either.

So, I went back and forth to work, and all during that time I would see a lot of that same brother who had visited me in the school and his wife. I would drop into their place or I would meet them for a drink in town, but, in a way, I was always glad to get back to the safety of the hostel. There was always somebody there doing something, and at least we were used to one another. We paid a minimal rent, and our food was all cooked for us. The door was always open, but you were expected to be back at a certain time.

Then I met the man I was to marry. I was working in the restaurant, and he would come in for lunch. At the time, things weren't going that well for me at the hostel. I had started to go out more, and this led to rows. You see, in the school we all played by the same set of rules, but when I went out into the world, I came to realise that people can manipulate you. People might think you are stupid and take advantage of you even with money and so on. Myself, and probably a lot of girls like me, we allowed ourselves to be used and manipulated by men.

The nuns never told us the facts of life. They never told us about dealing with men when you leave school. It's a big shock when you think somebody likes you or loves you only to find that they couldn't care less. I know girls of my own age now would be much more aware and knowledgeable. I know Catriona [daughter] would never allow someone to treat her like I was treated. Her environment is different. She is out in the world. She saw my situation and what happened to me, so she has some understanding of it. In school we didn't know where babies came from. We didn't know anything. Then you are thrown out in the world and you are landed with one yourself, and you have to cope. Sometimes the world can seem quite cruel when you leave a school like that.

I got married fairly young. I had a row in the hostel. At the time it was quite major, because I decided to go and live with this man who became my husband. The nuns were saying, "You can't leave, you are not long left the school." But I was just really lonely. Even though I knew the other girls in the hostel, sometimes I'd think, "Is this going to be my life for ever?" Two of the girls in the hostel, who had been there while I was still at school, were still in the hostel five years on. They depended on the nuns for everything, and I thought, "My God, I don't want this." They didn't seem to be able to cope in an environment outside of the school, and I was afraid that I would become institutionalised like that. I knew that I had some capability, but my shyness and my insecurity held me back. I felt that my opinion didn't matter because I didn't matter. I couldn't voice what I felt or what I wanted. Then, when I did, I went about it in the wrong way.

I stayed with the marriage for nine years. There were some good times, but more often than not it was very unhappy. My husband didn't socialise, and he didn't feel that I should socialise either. I was very isolated in my marriage, very cut off. Even though we lived in a big estate with houses on either side of us, I was still very much on my own with a baby, and there was little or no communication outside. And the feeling of being so alone didn't help if you have a husband who reminds you of who you are and where you went to school and that you can't get by in the world, that you need him for everything. If somebody tells you this continually, well, gradually you begin to believe it; until one morning you wake up and say, "Well, bloody hell, I just better try and manage, hadn't I?" When I left my marriage, I didn't have anything. I left with the two little girls and just the clothes on our backs.

Family ties

I was very close to that particular brother who had come with my mother to the school that day. Afterwards he continued to visit us on his own and was quite good to me. Through talking to him, I got to know about other members of the family. I was a bit hesitant to ask questions, but if he was willing to give the information, I was willing to listen. He didn't know very much about my childhood because he is just a few years older than me. He said, "When I was young, I often remembered being at home and giving you your bottle. You were a little black baby, and suddenly you disappeared and nobody ever spoke about you again." He said I might have had a twin as he remembered this other little black baby in the house and how he died of some disease. After meeting him a few times, he introduced me to one of my sisters, Anna. She was very chuffed to meet me and was very nice, but she didn't really speak much about the family. She was quite shy. Later my brother introduced me to his girlfriend, who is now his wife. After I left the school and moved to the hostel, my brother would call now and again to check that I was all right, but I didn't see as much of him then. The odd weekend I would go up and stay with him.

When I met the man who became my husband, I gradually began to lose contact with my brother. My sister had moved and was living somewhere else, so I had kind of lost touch with her. Now and again I'd ring her where she worked, but I wouldn't see her as often. My brother moved jobs and he and his wife moved further away, so I saw less of them as well. My husband wasn't inclined to let me see much of my family, so on and off the only contact I would have were the occasional phone calls. When my daughter, Caitriona, was born, we had a christening party, and my brother was her godfather. When she made her communion, he and his wife came to the house, and the same with my younger daughter. I would go to their houses for special occasions, but I didn't see as much of either of them as before.

At one stage, things were pretty bad in my marriage. On a few occasions I left, and I used to go back to the school where I was brought up. The nuns were good to me. They took care of me and gave me the time to decide what I wanted to do. I felt I couldn't communicate with my husband, and the nuns encouraged me to stay with them until I decided what to do. One of the nuns in particular said to me, "Whatever you decide to do, whether you want to stay in the marriage or not, we will support you." They were good to me, and I always went back to my husband, of course.

On one of those occasions, when I did leave, I decided that I would make a break for good. Instead of going to them, I thought I would try and go it alone and find a flat. I rang my brother, and he said he would introduce me to this other brother. If I was sure that this was what I wanted to do, he would help me to pack and find a flat; this other brother helped me move, and I settled into my little flat with Caitriona.

It lasted about a week, I would say, but during that week, sitting there alone, feeling really down and sad and lonely, I decided I needed a family. For some reason, I decided I would ring my father. I had never met him, but I had often heard my brother say that he worked in one of the embassies, so I asked the woman upstairs if she would come down and stay with Caitriona while I went to the phone. She agreed, so I phoned the embassy and asked for my father and was told that he was out but would be back later. I rang again and then I was put through to him. I said, "I am sure you are going to be very shocked, but I am your daughter, Caroline." There was a long silence. I said, "Are you there?"

He said, "Yes, I am still here." Then he said, "What do you want?" a bit nervously. I began to cry. I broke down and said, "I am really on my own, I've left my husband and I just feel really bad and I really want somebody." He just said, "Well, I can't talk to you now, I am busy. Could you ring me again? Give me two days and phone me back then."

I had butterflies in my tummy at the fact that I actually spoke to him, but in my heart I felt sad. It took a lot of courage, and I was tempted, while I was waiting for him to come to the phone and again when I first heard his voice, to put the phone down. I thought, *I am about to speak to the man whom I think is my father*. But because I had waited so long, I had to go ahead. I might never get the opportunity again. I felt sad when his response was so negative, but I thought I would phone again.

In the meantime, I got to the point where I couldn't stick the flat, and I phoned my husband and told him where we were staying. He said, "I knew you'd come back." And we went back home.

We had moved to Howth. One day shortly after that, I was rooting through my bag. I came across this phone number, and I decided, *I'll ring Dad*. When I was put through, one of the first things he said was, "You gave me an awful fright the last day."

I said, "I just want to see you and talk to you and Mum."

I told him I was back with my husband, and he said that he was glad about that. He arranged to come and visit the following Sunday. I was really excited. My husband didn't know that I had contacted my father. That evening when he came from work, I told him about the visit.

He said, "What the hell do you think you are doing? That family was never any good to you. You should leave all that behind you." He was really angry. I just said that it was all arranged and he didn't have to be there when my father came.

Sunday came. We were living in a beautiful house overlooking the sea. My husband was actually at home that afternoon. I kept looking out at every car that went by, thinking, *Is this him?* because I had no idea what he looked like. Finally, this white car pulled up and an elderly man got out. I thought, *That must be him*, so I went to the door. This man stood there and said, "Hello, Caroline." I just rushed to him and put my arms around him and hugged him, and he said, "Oh, mind, I've got rheumatism."

Automatically I jumped back and I said, in my own mind, *This isn't going to work.* I just said to him, "Sorry about that. Welcome to our house."

He was in his fifties and had very blue eyes. He must have been quite handsome when he was young. We talked, or rather made small talk — my husband, my father and I. He met Caitriona and he thought she was lovely. I said, "It's great to have you here." I didn't know what to say actually. We didn't talk about the family or anything. I just said that I had met my brother and my sister, Anna, and I asked how they were, and he said that they were fine and told me the names of the other brothers and sisters.

At some point I said, "You have lovely blue eyes and mine are so dark." I also asked if he had been away on holidays because he was really tanned, but I discovered he had been ill and his colour was due to his illness. I was really thinking that the meeting wasn't going too well and that I kept putting my foot in it. Later I asked him if he was really my father. He said he was, and I just looked at his colour and my colour and thought, *That's strange*, but I didn't say any more about it at the time. I didn't feel close to him or anything, and the fact that he pushed me away at the beginning didn't help. I think, even today (although he no longer lives in this country) when I know him a bit better, I would never have been close to him.

He brought presents for us. Before he went, he said, "I have a letter here from your mum. She said she is sorry she couldn't come today. She was feeling ill, but she said to tell you she will call over in about two weeks' time."

Finally, he left. It was about 7pm and I felt really strange. I was shaking. I felt happy and I felt sad and I felt loads of different emotions. Then I started to cry. When my father was going to the door to leave, I said, "Please don't go." And he said that he had to go. So I gave him a hug. A gentle one this time.

After he left, I was looking at the lovely presents he had brought: a lovely coloured chain for me, from him and from my mum; a beautiful dress for Caitriona and lovely shoes and little socks; and a present for my husband. My husband came into me in the kitchen and said, "You shouldn't take anything from them." He was really angry and said, "I don't ever want to see him here again. They were never there for you." He was really harsh. He asked why I wanted to get involved with the family.

I always wanted Caitriona to have grandparents. I always wanted that because her other little friends all had grannies that would treat them like their special girl, and I wanted someone to appreciate her like I do. So I said to my husband, "I don't care what you say, my mum is coming over in two weeks and I want to meet her. If you don't want to be here, then don't."

I didn't hear from my mother, but I had the letter she sent me. Then one day Anna phoned me and said, "Caroline, I'm very sorry, but Mum died."

I said, "That can't be. You know how my father came out to the house and said that Mum was coming to see me." I started to fight with her on the phone, saying, "Don't be telling me things like that; I haven't met her yet."

Anna said she had died of a heart attack the day before. I asked her why she didn't phone and tell me immediately, and I said she might have wanted to say something to me. I said, "She had never spoken to me and you have had her all your lives. I never had a chance to get to know her or anything." So Anna rang off.

When my husband came in that evening, I told him. He didn't say anything. I think he actually shrugged his shoulders. He just said, "Stop that nonsense" when I was crying. I told him I was going to the funeral.

Later I rang the nuns in the school and asked them did they think it would be all right for me to go to the funeral. They said, "Of course. She is your mum. No matter what happened, you have a right to be there".

My sister rang back and told me the details. So, I went. My husband said we weren't going and then, at the last minute, said we were. When we got there, the rest of the family were up near the grave, but I decided to stay back a good bit from where they were. I felt so empty and distant. I just looked at them and thought, "I don't have my family; I don't have anybody." When the service was over my father came up to me. I think I said, "I'm sorry, Dad."

He said, "We will miss her." So I said, "I will miss her more because I never knew her. I will miss her most of all." My father said we were welcome to go back to the house with them, but we didn't go. We just came home. It was the saddest day ever. I don't think I ever had a day as sad as that. My husband never mentioned it. I cried for days and days after that. My husband was so hard. Even if he put his arms around me, but he never did that. It was like the end of a chapter in my life.

At one stage I was in hospital. I had become very ill, through my own doing really, and ended up in hospital. This would have been after my marriage breakdown. I went to the refuge in Rathmines and took the two girls with me. I used to sit in the bedroom. When the girls were asleep, I had time to think of my life and where it was going and where I had been; thinking about the marriage breakdown and not having a family. I thought of the situation and that this was going to be my life. I felt what my parents had, or rather hadn't done for me impinged on my life. I said to myself, *If my parents had been different, I probably would still be in my marriage.* Sitting there in the room, thinking about my life, I just got depressed. It was a very low point in my life. The reason I was in hospital was because I took an overdose. I thought, *Well, the girls might be happier without me.* My life was not really going anywhere and I had no support. I thought that maybe there was somebody who could take better care of them than me.

One day in the hospital I met my father again. He happened to be calling in to visit somebody he worked with. I met him walking along the corridor. He said, "What are you doing here? You look ill."

I said that I had been quite ill. He said that he was visiting a friend and was in a hurry. And I said to him, "Well, couldn't you spend some time with me? I am your daughter. I think I am more important."

So he said he would call when he had seen his friend. So he called back and said, "I can't stay in long because I am rushing. I have to go to work."

I said, "I don't have much to say to you really, but there is one thing I have to ask you. Are you my father? And why did you not keep me in the family?"

He just said, "Well, I'm not responsible for what you do with your life."

I said, "No, in a way that is true, but in another way you are responsible. Because your parents are your parents and what they decide to do with their child impinges on its future. Can you be truthful with me? I may never see you again, and you are always rushing around when I want to talk to you. So I just want to know, are you my father?"

He said, "Of course, I am. You are just thinking always of yourself. Go home, go back to your husband. I'm going to go now." And he left.

That was the only intimate conversation I had with my father, and he was very defensive. So with my father, I felt that avenue for finding out more about my childhood was closed off. He wouldn't or couldn't be honest with me, so I thought, *I will leave it.*

I left the refuge, and later when I moved to the house here, I got on with living. But every now and again — well, very often really — I would think and cry about the situation and my past. It was only through meeting James, my boyfriend, in the last year, when he said, "We will try and if you want we will pursue this." The option of getting information from the family was closed, so we approached the hospital, and starting from there I have found out about my whole life in a few short months.

Myself and James did the research, which took us to the Mater Hospital, where I found out that I had spent periods of time there as a young child. They have a research unit and were able to trace my records. We were going back and forth to them, and after a while, a professor wrote to me and asked if I would go in and have a chat with him. I went in to see him. James came with me. It was very interesting when he brought out this big brown envelope and said, "Caroline, these are your files. I hope you have support." Well, I had James with me, so the doctor then said, "These are for you. You can take them with you." The records were from the time I had stayed in the hospital. He warned me that they might be a bit upsetting to read.

The little "black baby"

We sat down there and went quickly through it, and I cried because I never knew of these early years in my life. At times, it seems, I went through a lot. I have no memory of it, so to see it written down on paper gave me a start. Reading through it, there are comments from my mother, from my father, comments from the social workers and from people who had got to know me in the hospital, and really it was harrowing reading.

I always wondered myself how I ended up going to Glenmaroon. My mother wasn't able to tell me, on that one brief time that I met her, and I wasn't mature enough to ask. When I was older and got to meet my father, he wasn't willing to give me the information. But it was all there in the records. When I was born and they saw my colour, my mother was shocked. She couldn't cope with my colour and had a breakdown. I did go home to the family, but it seemed she left me there for the others in the family to care for me. She dressed me and washed me and I was spotlessly clean, but she didn't hold me or hug me.

There is one report from a visiting social worker that is quite sad and disturbing. This social worker described how I was getting on with the family, and she said she saw this little black girl on the floor wiping traces of dust from the floor. That was my environment. She reported that I did not look at my mother and my mother never acknowledged the child on the floor. My mother said to the social worker that I wasn't reaching the normal milestones, and that when I should be sitting up, I wasn't sitting up, and I was behind the other children. They thought a spell in hospital might help to get it sorted out. While I was in hospital, I responded to the nurses and the doctors. I was actually beginning to gain weight. But, as soon as I went home, I started to go downhill again. On the second occasion that I went into hospital, it was discovered that I had lesions on my back. Nobody could account for them. They were septic and looked like they hadn't been attended to. The hospital said the lesions were neglected and that this contributed to my ill health. So I was sent back to hospital, and I began to gain weight again.

My mother and father then asked the social workers, would there be a possibility for me to be put away into a home? My mother was being ostracised by her family and neighbours because of the black child. The neighbours' children wouldn't play with my siblings because they had a black sister. My mother was finding it difficult to cope, and she felt that the problems within the family were caused by me. The social workers responded that there wasn't a place for me to go as I had family and parents; but, they said, if there was any sign of mental retardation, I could be sent to a special school. I feel my mother deliberately didn't bond with me and that affected my growth, which in turn affected my learning capability. I had no stimulation in the house. Or no love.

In one of the letters, my father is pleading with the social worker, saying, "We feel she is handicapped. Would you be able to take her in now?"

It was as though they were counting on me being handicapped, so they could find a way of getting rid of me.

I wrote to my father last year and asked him about some of the information I had got. I asked him to explain why they couldn't have kept me as I wasn't mentally ill or anything, and that with a bit of love and attention, I would have come on and been the same as the other children. I also asked him why I am black and the rest of family are white, and where did I fit in? I asked him again, "Are you my father?"

He phoned me and said, "I have told you over and over again I am your father. Your mother is your mother. As to why you were sent to the school — you were just not very bright and we had to put you into that school." He also said, "I can't explain your colour."

In one of the letters, the social worker wrote, "The parents seem to have a bond with one another and with the other children."

The professor at the hospital said that the origin of my colour is on my mother's side. It could be going back through generations, but they can't pinpoint exactly which generation. It may have skipped some generations and it was just me. Nobody explained that to my mother at the time. She was very young as well. She had a lot to cope with. I think if somebody explained this to her, she may have been a bit stronger.

They lived in an ordinary house, but my father always worked, and my mother worked outside the house as well. It seemed they always had a nice comfortable home, wherever they lived. My father worked very hard and was abroad quite a bit. He was a chauffeur. So as far as I know, this embarrassment over me wasn't a class thing. They were just ordinary people. Most people would not have any experience of that kind of situation. There mustn't have been too many black children around.

Another thing we learnt from this doctor at the hospital was about this brother who died. I thought I had a twin and that this twin was black. Nobody is sure if that was the case. My older brother said that there was another black child like me who died. I think that is how the idea of being a twin got into my head. He was called Albert. He died when he was three years old of kidney failure or liver disease, but nobody is sure whether his colour was caused by the disease or if he was actually black.

At one stage my mother and father wrote to the social worker, "We think Caroline's colour is the result of having the same disease that her brother Albert died of. We are hoping that is all her colour is." That is how they saw it.

The social worker commented, "This is a very sad case. It's sad to see parents using an illness to blame for the child's colour." Another comment she makes is, "The mother cannot see the colour in front of her eyes. She wants to deny that this exists." My mother could never accept it.

There is also an account from the social worker of going to the house and being introduced to other family members. My sister, Anna, was brought into the room where I was. Anna apparently began to play with me, and the social worker said, "Anna seems to get on well with Caroline." My mother replied, "Yes, I'm very happy that Caroline at least looks a little like her sister, Anna."

Self, affinities, identity

At school I didn't realise I was different. It seems strange, but I was never aware of my skin. As I got older, sometimes I'd see somebody on the TV and I would notice that they looked like me.

I think I suffer with depression. My doctor says I don't. In school, even though it was large, maybe a hundred and fifty or two hundred and I joined in all of the activities, I found that despite all the other kids, I always felt distant from them. I always liked to be on my own, especially as a teenager. I always remember staring out the window for long periods of time. Maybe it was because of being in the school, but I had to have space. There were times when I needed not to talk to anyone for days, and in a big school you can't get away without talking to anyone. I used to deliberately hold my mouth shut and wouldn't speak. I used to cut myself off.

In some ways my colour was an advantage to me at school, and in a way I feel I used my colour in quite a nasty way at times. I realise that now. Some of the girls would call me names, and, if I was feeling particularly nasty, I would say that they had even when they hadn't, just to get back at someone. I'd say, "Sister, she called me that," and the nun would lash out. And when visitors came to the school, I was always shown off by the nuns. I was always pushed forward. They would say things like, "Isn't she beautiful?" I was shy anyway, but that made me much more so.

Then there was this nun. She wasn't nice to me, and I didn't have much dealings with her, but sometimes I would be sent to help her. She never called me by my name. She would always call me "Darkie". I used to hold back the tears. She would say, "Darkie, come here," even though she knew my name. Now, she was old, so I suppose I have to take that into account, but there were other nuns who were older than her, and they always called me by my name. I think she couldn't accept me because she was from the country, and I was beneath them in her eyes: I didn't deserve to be called by my name.

While I was at the school, we used to go away on holidays down the country to places like Clifden and stay in bed and breakfast places; you could see people looking in amazement. I remember once there was these boys, and they came all the way across to shake my hand. I hated it because, afterwards, I could see them sniggering. I think they thought I couldn't talk.

I find some of the people around here treat me like that. It is like saying, "That thing can't talk." I had a lot of harassment from my neighbours. It was the parents mainly, and then the children copied them. It was hard for my older daughter. She was eight when we moved here to this house. It was hard for her having to leave home and be in the refuge and then to come here to all that.

I remember, too, when I was working as a waitress, there were these Americans in the restaurant, and I was looking after their table. I was chatting to them and they asked where I was from. I said, "Oh, I'm Irish." They started laughing then, and I could feel myself getting red. Then I realised that they must have thought that I was spoofing. So I said, "But I am, even if I don't look it." It was very embarrassing, but then I have a right to say it, because Ireland is my country. I don't know any other culture, so what could I say but that?

I feel it would have been better even if my parents had put me into an orphanage. In the school where I was, I only learnt the basic literacy and maths, and nothing more was expected of us. If you were brighter, and some of the girls were, and if circumstances were different, you wouldn't have been in a school like that; so I feel our parents were unfair. First, they gave us away. And then, they sent us to a school where you were stigmatised by handicap. You couldn't live it down.

Something like getting my birth certificate was very important for me. That bit of paper made such a difference. We had gone out for a meal with a friend to a pub. Then the barman announced my name and asked me to go to the bar to collect a package, which I did, although I was very embarrassed. I came back to the table and sat down and opened it, and it was my birth certificate. It was absolutely brilliant. James had arranged for it to be at the pub for me as a surprise. Before that I couldn't get a passport, and it was dreadful because your birth cert is your identity. If parents decide they are going to give you away, at least they should make sure that you have that basic right of citizenship. I feel in my case the fact that I didn't have any real identity was part of my being rejected.

I found when I left school and became aware of black people that I hated them. Before I left school, we used to watch this programme called "Roots", and I found it portrayed black people very negatively. It's funny, because now if I'm walking down the street, a black person will always give a wink or acknowledge you. I like that now. It is nice. Then, if somebody did that, I'd turn in disgust. I was ashamed. Now I'm more positive about it. For a while last year, I wanted to be involved in everything to do with black people. I was trying to find a place to fit in somewhere.

All the time when I didn't know my family, it wasn't that I wanted them to be rich or poor. I just wanted them to be — well, not what they are anyway. I just wanted them to be, or one of them to be, from Africa. Then I could feel that I was part of them and say, "One of my parents is from Africa." I feel very sad. I feel that I haven't found my family yet. They are my parents and they are my siblings, my blood brothers and sisters, but, at times, I feel I am still waiting. It makes me sad to feel that I haven't found them, because I know that I have.

Mike

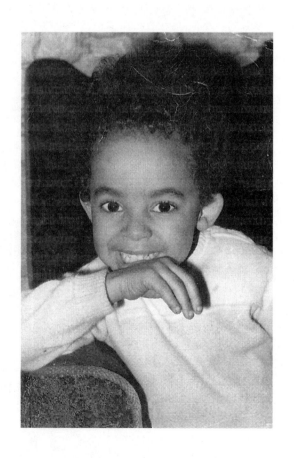

It is all to do with background.

Mike is the last born of a large family. His mother, Sarah, died when Mike was nineteen. During her marriage, she occasionally left the family home and went to stay with her sister as a respite from her husband's heavy drinking.

On one of these occasions, she met and fell in love with Samuel, from Zambia, who was on a study sabbatical in Dublin. Some time after, Sarah returned to the family home and Mike, Samuel's son, was born. During the next nine years, Samuel continued to correspond with Sarah. Mike has not yet read these letters, which were passed on to him by his aunt, but his wife, Lucy, has. Mike and Lucy are both Jehovah's Witnesses and have two young children.

Background and growing up

I grew up in a family of five boys and two girls, with six years between me and my brother. I was the baby and I was well looked after by the others. I'm thirty-four now, and when you think back to when I was growing up, times were hard and families had trouble making ends meet most of the time. Me da [stepfather] was fond of the old gargle, so at times it was a struggle for me ma. There were times at home when it wouldn't have been great, because when you have alcohol in an environment, you have all kinds of problems. In many ways it was happy, and in others it was traumatic for us kids.

Going back to that time, for men, especially working-class men, drink was part of the environment. All the men drank. Me da went for a few pints on his lunchtime most days, and he'd have a drink on his way home and then go back down to the pub in the night-time. That was just the way it was; it didn't seem unusual to us. He probably put more energy into drinking than he ever did into the home, but he had very good qualities as well. I believe, with hindsight, that his background played a big part in the man he turned out to be. He was brought up by his older brother and sister, as their parents died when they were very young. When they were growing up, they would have had a problem providing shoes and things like that. They were really poor and had a hard struggle, and he would have brought a lot of these experiences into his family life. I think he was about fourteen when his mother died. A hard age, a time when you really need your parents around you.

He could be very hard, but he had lovely ways about him as well and could show great softness. He was an emotional character at times. I have some really fond memories of him. We all do in different ways. But just sometimes you'd see the other side of him, and it would outweigh the nice side. On top of that, he gave me ma a hard time because of the drink. She struggled, and you could never say anything bad about her because she was an amazing woman in so many ways. The fact that she never gave me up speaks volumes about the type of person that she was. She was a tower of strength to all of us.

My father did what came natural to him. At times things would get out of hand, and he would hit her a clatter and she'd hit him back. I would have seen a good bit of that. Not all the time, but occasionally when they would have bad rows. Then he'd be the sorriest in the world. On a few occasions, she left him when she couldn't put up with it any longer. She'd make him pay in other ways by letting him know that he was out of order. There were a couple of major incidents over the years that stick out in my mind.

He made a lot of mistakes. He acted first, and hours later you might have a chance to tell him what had happened. I remember that's what happened on his fiftieth birthday. He came in from the pub that night and he was all emotional, but I wasn't having any of it because earlier that day I had got a box in the mouth for nothing from him. In those days, all of the men from our walk of life would have been like that, beating their kids. That's why you see so many young fellas now who have problems with their own children, because they don't know how to deal with them. I believe quite a lot would have grown up in a violent environment and would be violent with their own children now.

With us there was no half measures. That's the way I was raised by the boys in our house. When I was a kid, if somebody did something to me, I couldn't go into my house and say somebody was after hitting me. I'd be told, "Go out and hit them." Now my mother wasn't like that. My father wasn't really like that either, but he used to knock the boys around a lot. He was a tailor, and he'd take the strap off the machine, and I remember him beating David with it when David was a kid. When my da hit you, he really hurt you. But he was a street angel. I probably got the least of it because my mother protected me. What I got I remember, so I can imagine what it was like for the other boys.

In most of the households of working-class Dublin, the mother was a bit of a second-class citizen. My mother was probably a stronger kind of woman than most.

Growing up, apprenticeship and London
Loads of times in the past, when I'd be with my mates, I'd have racist things said to me. Before I was driving, I might be going on a bus to meet somebody, and I'd meet it on the bus. There would be a load of fellas down the back of the bus. I'd walk upstairs, and they'd be down the back chanting things like, "Hey, nigger boy, what do you do when the sun goes down?" You know, all that kind of

thing. Then me and my mates would run amok, and I'd get into rows over it. We'd just burst people. When I was growing up, because I came from a rough background, I always carried weapons. I'd always have a Stanley knife or a blade. I was the type of individual that if anyone messed with me, I would have given it to them. Back then, I did some bad things, but that is all in the past. I was wild at the time.

They'd always be stunned when I'd open my mouth and they'd realise I was a Dublin bloke. It was funny really. People always assume when they see you that you are from a different country, especially when I was growing up here. There wouldn't have been so many different nationalities as there are now. Now in Blanchardstown the place is packed with people from Bosnia and Nigeria and else-where, but back then there was nothing like that.

My older sister married a man from Zambia. I was prob-ably about nine years old when this brother-in-law from Zambia came on the scene. I was twelve when my niece was born. It was probably a coincidence for my sister to marry a Zambian man. I'm not sure, but I think that me being around could have opened her up to being more accepting, and that might have influenced her choice of husband. There were no problems, and he was very well liked by all the family. I got to meet all his friends, so I was lucky in that respect. My sister lived in Zambia for a time, which was a bit unusual back then, as it seemed so remote and commu-nications weren't as good as they are nowadays.

When I left school I went to ANCO for training. My sis-ters knew one of the instructors there, a lovely fella called John. I got into welding and went straight into a job. John told me that if I kept my head down and did my work, he'd help me find a job; so I served my time and he did. I never finished the apprenticeship as the place closed down. I was there for three years, and then it went bust. I went to another place where I stayed for about six months, and then I got out of it altogether. After that, I was labouring and doing bits and pieces, and then I went across to England and worked for a while over there. I was in a place called Willesden, and I used to dance in the Camden Palace at weekends, but I didn't like London. I was working in McVities with people from all different backgrounds. I feel the West Indian people were much warmer than English people. I remember a man called Ali, who was from Pakistan, and myself and Ken (who went over with me) would have the *craic* with him; even though Ken was white, it made no difference to Ali. Me and Ken would mix with anyone who would have the *craic* with us, but the English people couldn't even get drunk without getting narky. We'd be falling about the place laughing, and they would have a few pints on them and be wanting to fight everyone. So no, I didn't really like England at all. I missed the family terrible and I missed Lucy. I was about twenty-one when I met Lucy, and I had gone to London to find work to get a few things together and do the things we planned to do.

I had my own circle of friends in Dublin, a wide circle of friends. I've always known that where my friends were concerned I was held in high esteem, which is a nice thing to know. When I came back to Dublin, I was out of work for a while; I was back on the labour. Then I went to work in a hotel after about a year and have been there about ten years now.

Mother and (step)father's relationship
My mother is dead about twelve or thirteen years now. I am brutal with years. I can never remember year to year. You see, everyone tells me that I don't look my age, so I don't care about time. I couldn't tell you what year me da died, and that's not a bad thing. Things that I don't want

to remember, I just shut down in my mind. Anyway, my mother was never very well. She used to be good at times. Of course, we didn't understand about stress back then. There were a few blow-ups, and Ma would end up in hospital over it. And we played our parts in the lifestyles we led in making her life harder.

Ma had been born with a rare murmur in her heart. She was a doctor's delight, as they found out things about that type of murmur from her going into hospital so often; it was an opportunity for them to try different treatments out. There was barely a year that I remember that she wasn't in hospital at least once. She had a number of operations on her heart. She developed a bowel problem that was cured by a certain diet. But while her own doctor was away, she got very sick, and it was decided to operate, but she had a massive stroke shortly after the operation and she was dead by the Sunday.

We were very upset because as far as we were concerned it was a mistake on their part. We could have done something about it, but it wouldn't have brought me ma back, and no amount of money would have replaced her. So we let it go. She was only fifty-six when she died.

It happened a couple of times that I remember that things got bad and she left to go to her sister's, but she always took me with her. She loved all of us the same, but I was the baby, and it would have been hard to take all seven kids. Probably, in the back of her mind, she thought about the circumstances that brought me about. It's possible that at some stage me da would have resented me. I don't remember it, but it's possible.

Me da drank before he married and all through his life, though he went off it a few times for Lent. I think he realised in his heart that he had a wonderful woman and he did love her. It reminds me that I'm a very lucky man to have met Lucy. Lucy and I are different in many ways. I recognise that I have similar qualities that my da had, and when I think of that I realise how lucky I am now.

But me da never really realised how lucky he was. Maybe he was so far gone with the drink. I'm not sure.

I know when she died he did realise what he had lost. I was living in the house at that time, and you couldn't touch anything in the house. I remember needing a bit of space for some of my gear. I cleared out one of the drawers, and I remember about three days later he discovered that and he went mad.

"Why didn't you leave things the way they were? The way your mother had them!"

He was drinking so much at that time that it caused a lot of problems between the two of us. It caused him so many problems. I was young and I was dealing with my own grief, and the only way I knew was to fight him. I ended up nearly killing him, and that's how I came to leave the house. I couldn't take it any more. A friend of mine actually stopped me from killing him. I realised then that I could never stay in the same house with him again, but, of course, we made it up afterwards. I have things in me mind about me da, little jokes and things like that, and there will always be my relationship with him. I have no bitterness in my heart against him. Not now, because I can understand why he was the way he was. But I would never have been born if things had been right for her. She would never have been unfaithful if her marriage had been different.

In her last few months, they had a brilliant relationship. She was sleeping downstairs the night she had the stroke. During those months, he looked after her so well. That night she took the stroke, she was saying to him, "Tom, you go down the road and have a drink," and he said, "No, I'm fine, I'm fine." In the end he did go down, and he came back to find her lying by the fireplace. Me ma had really long hair, and if he hadn't come in at that time she would have been burnt. But that last time was great. It shows you what could have been. They got on so well, and it's great for all of us to be able to look back at that time.

My biggest regret is that Lucy never got to meet her, because I can talk about her all I like but she was already dead when Lucy and I met, and she was a wonderful woman. Me ma was amazing, and everybody loved her. She was also fairly private. If you told her something, nobody ever heard it from her. She came from a very well-to-do background, completely different from my father. Her family were the only people on the Phibsboro' Road to have a car, and they owned a shop and lived in a big four-storey house.

I'm realistic and admit me da was reeking with problems, but all the family are very close and loving. All the good qualities that we have come from me ma. If we had the right backing, we could have done a lot better in our relationships and in our lives.

Relationships

I think my colour made it easier meeting girls. I never had any problem meeting girls in any shape or form. Once you'd go down to the pub, you'd be sitting down and you'd be more interested in having a drink when some girls would be over talking to you. If I was talking to people, I'd always have a bit of a laugh, and people would think I was a happy-go-lucky sort of a person, but I have experienced racism there, too.

Even though I hear stories of bad experiences from my niece, who is half Zambian, I think it's worse for men than it is for women. It's always different when you meet the parents. This was even true with Lucy's father when we started going steady. I'd never hold that against him, but he was concerned for his daughter. He said at one stage, "I never thought I was racist or anything, but it's completely different when it's your daughter." Then other things come into play because you begin to think how other people might view the situation — maybe Lucy's friends or her granny. We met her granny on the bus one day and we got on very well together. I thought she was really nice, and it was my first time meeting her. Then later on the granny turned around to Lucy and said, "He's a lovely chap, but you could do better." Why should she say that?

I've had experience of the same kind of thing on numerous occasions. It was a bit more extreme with Lucy's mother. She came straight out with some really hurtful kind of things about me to Lucy. She probably didn't perceive them as racist, but they were. At the time I was younger and it wasn't very nice. It's as if they didn't see me as a human being with feelings. But we all get on really well now.

For months I refused to go to Lucy's house and meet her parents. She'd say, "Come on," and I'd refuse and she would ask why. I'd tell her that when I would go to her house I'd get loads of hassle off her parents. She didn't believe it, but I had experienced it so many times. And I was right. They didn't know anything about my wild side and I had always known how to behave in different circumstances. I don't mean to imply that I would act like a hypocrite. It's like, even in the job I am in now, I'm just an ordinary Dublin fella, but I can mix with the best of people. I became very wise at adapting to different social situations. I pick up people's vibes. For me it's like second nature to do that. I've always been a very good judge of character. Not all of the time, but most of the time, I get it right.

The first night I went up to the house, I heard from Lucy later that they thought I was quite nice. I was very respectful and mannerly and I didn't take anything for granted. They had to say, "Well, he's a very nice bloke." Then they noticed that I wasn't working, so they were able to use that as an excuse, as if "It's not that he's black or anything, but we'd be like that with anyone who wasn't working." To me it was all crap. It was just an excuse. For me it was all about colour, because if it was just about a job, why should they attack your character?

The Bible and change

The biggest change in my life came from studying the Bible. If that hadn't happened, I'd be locked up now or in some other kind of prison by this time. This is the only reason why I changed. I know I have it in me to love kids. I have a really good relationship with all my nephews and nieces and my own kids, and I know they all love me because they are really affectionate with me, even the ones I don't see too often, but I know that before I became a Witness, I would have been violent. I always know that, in the past, if I got into a confrontation or something like that, I'd be inclined to try really to do damage to the other person. I always had a conscience, but I could justify doing a lot of wrong things at the same time.

But as well as that, I knew that there was more to life. People often look at the likes of myself and use the term "broken home" because of all the mixed-up lifestyle my family had. There is no doubt about it that we came from a very loving environment in many ways but a very troubled one at the same time. I suppose I was always searching for something more.

I picked up a cutting I had from an old newspaper the other day. I had assaulted a policeman. I had also bitten this fella's ear off. It sounds bad now, but everyone I knew was wild like that. My brothers are still like that — at least some of them are. Some of the fellas that I would have known then are dead or strung out on gear; other fellas are involved in crime. Generally, most people have problems. Some people might be married with a couple of kids, but they would still go off with another woman given the opportunity because they are not all right in themselves or they can't commit themselves to a proper family environment because of their own background. I'm more sorted out than them, maybe not in a material sense but in a spiritual way, and with my wife and family. Lucy and I have a wonderful relationship. I'm still fairly violent — not here at home or with Lucy or anything, but it's still part of me. It's still something I struggle with. Lucy's great for settling me down, because at times I can get boisterous with the kids when I don't mean it. I could fly off the handle for very little reason. Lucy talks to me and makes me see what's happening. So I have everything going for me in that way.

I was open-minded. I spoke to the Mormons first, and I worked out that what they were telling me just wasn't correct. When I spoke to the Witnesses, I checked it out for over a year. One day a man from Theresa's Gardens knocked on the door. He came from a troubled background himself, but after he became a Witness he changed completely and did things like knock drink on the head. I was still wild at that time, so I set out to trap him. Lucy was more into it than I was at first. I looked up some books to see if I could prove him wrong. When I found out that I couldn't, it really whetted my appetite. It took a while for things to change. It took time for me to suss it out.

I know myself that if I hadn't studied the Bible my kids would be destroyed — I have no doubt in my mind about that — because I'd have all sorts of people in the house. I'd be smoking blow all the time. I'd be drinking my head off. I'd be in bits as I'd be more concerned about drinking at the weekend. I'd be saying, "I've been working all the week. I have to get out." My priorities would be all over the place. That's if Lucy was still here, because she comes from a different background and wouldn't be used to that.

Work

Fellas whom I work with have seen how racist it can be for me and some of the things that happen to me on a regular basis. In the hotel, we do door duty as well. After a certain time of night, we direct everyone to one of the side doors. That way we have more control over the situation, because you never know who is coming up to the door. That way we can establish which people are staying in the hotel. You can't have every Tom, Dick or Harry coming into the hotel at that time of night for a drink. Some of the time you'll get people messing. I've had a few experiences on the door. They will say, "Get away, you black bastard," or whatever because I wouldn't let them in.

One night there were these people outside the door for ages and ages, and I had to go out to them. They were very abusive, but it goes in one ear and out the other with me. There are times when we've had people over from South Africa, from the Rugby Board. They were very condescending, really obnoxious people. One of the others [staff] came up to me and said, "Mike, you don't want to go in there. They are a horrible crowd." I went in anyway, and when I did what I got was somebody clicking his fingers, shouting to me, "Help, help," as if I was the hired help. He didn't get served for a long time. We were all laughing. You get that a lot. On the other hand, we all get on very well at work. The people I work with are quite protective of me, which is nice.

Irish and African cultures

I often compare Irish people to African people. It's to do with tradition and culture and being involved with music. When you go to Africa, there is a whole sense of community, and everyone knows everyone else. In Ireland, up to recently anyway, it was very similar. Now when you go to England and Germany and countries like that, tradition is gone. They have lost the sense of being in touch with their roots, being close to their neighbours. That's why tourists who come here all want to go to things like traditional sessions. They like the idea of the Irish being happy-go-lucky and being talkative and friendly.

If you go into a pub here and go up to the bar, it's likely that someone you've never met before will speak to you. That would never happen in England. I was talking to a taxi driver that I know the other night, telling him about our trip to the States, and he said, "Mike, in the States they are going to love you. They are going to be stunned first when you open your mouth." I see that when I meet Americans here. They say, "Hey, where are you from?"

I say, "Dublin," and my accent alone stops them in their tracks.

Me and my cousin often sing in the [hotel] lounge together, and groups come back for the sessions in the resident's bar. New Year's Eve we had a session there that was unbelievable. This year we got a load of Scottish people who came back from last year. We play everything: "Mac the Knife" and "Hey, Jude" and songs from the Dubliners and Christy Moore. People keep coming back and they are knocked out by it. The Americans who invited me over [to the States] are coming back to Dublin this year and will be coming across to the lounge for a session.

It's just the spontaneity of the cultural thing here. I've loads of friends that get up and do a knockout tune. They bang it out on a *bodhrán*. Lucy picks up the whistle. How many people do you know that can get up and play or sing, even if it's not in a very professional way? We all know somebody, and not just one person but a number of people, who can do this. I remember parties in my own house as a child. Our house was a great place for parties, and all the aunts and uncles would be there. Someone would take out the accordion, somebody else would have a whistle, and there would be a session to beat the band.

The European people haven't got that. The African people still do. They work with songs. You can see it in the cultural side; it's more artistic, more people involved and more self-expression. The unfortunate thing is they haven't got it across the water. You probably get pockets of it in parts of France where traditions are still alive. On the whole, for a country of our size tradition is still alive, although the sense of community is, to an extent, dying in the cities.

It has to be said that in this country people have more time for each other. It mightn't be the same as when we were young when you'd get a cup of sugar off your neighbour and you'd never be stuck, but people still speak to each other. You could be trying something on in a shop and somebody going by, somebody you've never met before, might say, "That's lovely on you." That sense of familiarity is still there. Waiting in a bus queue, somebody will strike up a conversation with you. Sitting on the bus, you're reading the paper, and somebody will lean over you saying, "That's terrible, isn't it?" That goes on right throughout the country. When that goes and we become like the other countries, it will be a sad day, because we will be much poorer.

Race, racism and identity

I'd always refer to myself as black. I don't believe in being half this and half that. Very definitely I see myself as being black, and that's very important to me. Nationally I'd call myself African–Irish. I find some terms offensive: the word "nigger" when used by white people. When black people use it, it's as a term of affection and isn't offensive. Words like "coloured" or "half-caste" are used, I think, more out of ignorance, and I find these terms annoying but not offensive.

I definitely feel an affinity with black people. I feel a lot more comfortable in the company of other black people. I find them more relaxed and happy, and they don't have the same hang-ups that white people have. I'd feel an affinity with anyone who is dark, especially in this country. Outsiders would tend to class us as the same, or it's presumed that there is some connection between us, but I don't have any problem with that.

When I was younger, if I showed interest in things that were African, people would say, "But you're not really dark," or things like that. I found that very annoying, but it stopped me from looking for the African side of myself, and it kept me back as a person. I didn't stand up for myself, and it was like that right through my twenties, until my early thirties. It stunted me as a person, and I didn't mature because that part of myself that was African and part of my sense of self and my identity was held back and wasn't resolved until quite recently. Now I find it very easy to have access to African music, to people and to the culture of Africa, and I'd get quite angry if people try to say that I'm not part of all of that.

I experience racism due to my colour quite a lot. At work you get it if you are serving at tables. You get people calling you "Manuel", and sometimes it's very obvious that people don't want to be served by me. If I'm handing somebody change, I often find they will withdraw their hand because they don't want to make contact. I always put those reactions down to my colour. Sometimes it's really blatant and people don't disguise it. Other times, people are condescending, looking down. In their minds it's obvious that they see me as "the boy", even though they don't say those words out loud. Other times again, people pretend to like you until it comes down to situations like where you are going out with their daughter, and then the issue of colour comes up again. I've experienced racism in numerous situations over and over. People are like sheep. They follow one another, so you can expect the same reaction from a certain number of people. We also find it in social situations when I am going out with Lucy and we are refused at the door. This happens more often than not. Lucy gets upset, but I have come to expect it. The way I deal with it depends on how bad it is. If people are blatantly racist, I might feel like hitting them. If they are condescending or patronising to me, I react in the same way towards them; it's difficult not to.

Racism in this country is getting worse. The media haven't helped. It's something Irish people are confronted with for the first time, and people are being forced to deal with it. It's going to get worse in this country. I think there should be more of an effort made to integrate people coming to Ireland. You have places like Brixton, in London, where people are all pushed into one area and there is no integration. Of course, this is going to create a "them" and "us" situation. It's creating more slums. We have to learn from the mistakes of others. You don't want to have "Bosnian" areas and "Nigerian" areas where people are ghettoised and the target of racism, but that's the way it is at the moment.

I think my children will definitely face some form of hardship on account of my colour. You always have people asking things like, "Where is their father from?" or "Their father can't be Irish." It's obvious that this will be an issue for them, but being part of the Witnesses has been fabulous for them in that there is no racism in the congregation. The children have got to know people from all walks of life through the congregation, so they have become quite balanced in that regard.

Samuel
Every day I think about my colour. I know that some day I'll get the money together so we can all go over there [Zambia] and search. I only have second-hand information

about my father. My mother was dead by the time I had all these questions, and my auntie knew very little. The letters from Samuel to my mother were there. I've never read them yet. Lucy has. In the letters it looks like Samuel was very wrapped up with my mother and loved her. I think if she didn't have the other children, she would have gone with Samuel, but she loved her children so very much that she wouldn't leave them.

I know Samuel wrote to her until I was seven or eight years of age. I will read the letters, but it's another step for me in sorting myself out. I want to read them, but, at the same time, I feel that I'm prying into me ma's business. She was a very private person in many ways, and I'm not comfortable about reading her private letters.

I hear myself say, "The man I call me da." He is me da. I mean Samuel is me da, but I'll never have the same relationship with him. I think I could have had a very close relationship with Samuel when I was growing up, but there are things that he'd never have known about me because he wasn't there. I think, when I was younger, my mother had planned to talk to me about her relationship with Samuel. The letters she had received from Samuel are there for me to refer to, and I believe at a later stage she planned to sit down and go over the letters with me. If she hadn't died when she did, I think it would have been easier for me to put the pieces of my life together. And if she hadn't died when she did, I believe I would have met my father a long time ago, and I would be a lot more knowledgeable about myself, but she had never talked to me about it. Probably she saw at the time that I was a troubled young fellow and she was waiting for me to grow out of the stage I was in. I don't think it was a case of her concealing things or of her leaving me in the dark out of badness. It was just that she died prematurely.

Lucy adds: Mike was just nineteen when his mother died, and it was just a few weeks later that his sister asked him, "Do you ever think of Samuel?" He said, "Samuel who?"

That was the first time that he had heard Samuel's name, let alone that he was his father. He was really gutted and very angry. Sarah had told the other children, or at least the older ones. It sounded like they knew all about him. It was hard for him finding out at the time. He got into trouble with the police and everything, and you can understand that. He had no one to ask about it.

Samuel had been a mature student studying politics and had come to Ireland as part of his training. When he went back [we since found out], he was district governor in his part of Zambia. Samuel had to go back to Zambia when Sarah was at the early stage of her pregnancy, but he promised she was going to follow him.

When she gave birth, he was excited about the baby and eager to hear from her, and as soon as Mike was born, money was being sent over. Samuel sent a card when Mike was born and in it he scribbled out "your little treasure" and put "our little treasure". He sent cards and presents and all these kinds of things. He thought she wasn't married and that this was her first child, so he was over there thinking, "Great, she's going to come over here with my son." For some reason he was never able to get back to Ireland, but he was writing for nine years.

All the letters went to Sarah's sister's house, Mike's aunt. She doesn't really like to talk about it much, as though it's still Sarah's secret, and we have to respect that. Mike's aunt met Samuel. She says he was very like Mike, only a little taller. She says he was "a quiet gentleman".

There were things in the letter like, "You're a lovely lady, honest and sincere," which, according to what everyone says, Sarah was. It must have been out of character for her to deceive somebody in this way, but she probably just loved Samuel so much. That is probably why she found it hard to write and explain to him. He trusted her so much, and in the letters he said that he loved her deeply.

Samuel, himself, was married at that time. It is customary in some parts of Africa for a man to have more than one wife if he chooses to do so. A few years after Mike was born, there was a letter for Sarah from a woman in England. She and her husband knew Samuel and had stayed in his house in Zambia, and she wrote to Sarah saying, "He never stopped talking about you and your son. He's really hoping that you can come over to see him."

She arranged to meet Sarah in England. There is another letter where she changes the date for the meeting, so Sarah obviously went to meet her. Mike remembers going to England a few times as a little boy with just his mother and it being his special time. That was one of the last letters. This woman was going back to visit Zambia, and I suppose she wanted to bring Samuel some good news. In my mind, Sarah told her the truth and she in turn told Samuel, and there were no more letters after that. Right up to that time, year after year, there are many letters, fifteen letters in the first nine years that we can trace; possibly there were more. Then they suddenly stopped. Maybe Sarah told the truth, and maybe Samuel, out of love of Sarah, decided to leave things alone. Or maybe he got angry and his love died. We don't know.

When Mike was born, Sarah was in her forties, but apparently she never looked her age. She was a very elegant and glamorous woman. Tom [stepfather] wouldn't have known that she was pregnant when she returned to the family home. It wasn't a matter of Tom accepting her back. He wanted her back. She left him because of the drink and selling everything around him. She went back on her own terms. I don't know if she knew she was pregnant or whether she started having relations with him again and went through with the pregnancy thinking nothing until the baby was born. We are told that when Mike was born, Tom didn't bat an eyelid about his colour. He probably thought, "Well, I haven't been a good husband so I can't say anything," and never questioned her or never let anybody else question her. Obviously I don't know what he felt inside, but when I knew him he treated Mike exactly like all the rest of the children; but it was Sarah's baby, and she thought of him as her baby and not Tom's. Tom wasn't allowed to discipline him in the way he did with the others, although he tried when she wasn't around. Tom loved Mike. He called him "Muruchu" as a pet name, and he had a special fondness for him. He wasn't the worst person in the world; it was just bad communication between the two of them. His background was very tough, and that's why Mike is not bitter, because he understands why Tom was like that.

Tom passed away four years after Sarah died. Those four years were full of tension building up and a lot of fighting. He treated Mike like a child, telling him to go to bed when Mike was twenty-one. When we became Jehovah's Witnesses, we both changed in our attitudes towards things. Tom felt it was good for Mike and was happy for him. Round about that time, I found out I was pregnant, and he was delighted about that.

It must have been very hard for Sarah. She was in a situation that nobody would wish to be in, and her best way of coping was to be strong. But for her not to tell Mike was terrible. He was angry with his mother for a long time. He had some therapy for it. He wrote some letters to her, even though she was no longer around, just to get it off his chest, because, you see, he loved her so much. Everyone was saying, "Mammy was lovely," but he was very angry with her. It came to a head with him. She of all people should have understood how hard it would be for him, going around and getting hassled for being a different colour, but he's over it now.

When he was born, it was obvious that he was black. When his sister went to school the next day and the nun asked about him, she said, "She [Sarah] had a black baby," but the family forgot about it, accepted him and never really talked about it. He didn't start to really think about his colour until he was about nineteen years old. People would ask him, "Why are you that colour?" but he'd just make a joke of it. Friends of the family treated him the same as the other children, but not everyone did. He does remember a birthday party was announced, and all the children ran into the house where it was to be held. As Mike ran in, all of a sudden a hand was put out to stop him, and he wasn't allowed in, for no reason except for the fact that he had a different colour skin. So he remembers things like that. Part of him knew there was something in him that meant he was different and drawn to black people, but because nobody ever said anything, he didn't want to ask and to appear foolish.

I wish he would read the letters and they would help him to see the type of man that Samuel was. He was a lovely man. I've read them and they are not love letters, but every second line he refers to Mike as "my son". That love that he shows never changed in all those years.

Lisa

IN MY MIND, I WAS ALWAYS "LISA THE DANCER".

Lisa lives with her husband and four teenage children in Bally-fermot, west Dublin.

Her bright and bubbly personality means she is popular with the customers who frequent the shop where she works. She tell the story of one elderly man who joked that his house was full of bread but he had to find an excuse to see her.

Lisa was adopted by relatives, but now both her adoptive parents and her natural mother are dead, and she has little knowledge of her natural father whom she believes is Ghanaian.

The child

I was adopted into my own family. My mother was working in England. She was very young and, unfortunately, got pregnant and didn't really know what to do, so she wrote and told my grandfather her news. I think she must have written to him after I was born, because all the way through her pregnancy it seemed that she was going to have me adopted. Then, after I was born, being very emotional and everything, she felt she couldn't go through with it, so she wrote her letter home. As a result, her brother and sister, who both had families of their own at the time, went over and brought me back to Dublin.

Now, I'm not completely sure of all the details. Remember, I was only three months old then. It's possible that my mother came back with me to Ireland to settle me in (I'm not sure), but soon after I know I went to live with my aunt who had travelled to England to collect me. My aunt had two daughters, and, even to this day, they regard me almost as a sister.

Then my aunt got ill and wasn't able to look after me, and when I was about six years old I went to stay in my grandmother's house. I have a very clear memory of being there in the house one day. In my granny's house, there were no children, just her son, and he was much older; and after being with my two cousins, I felt strange in those surroundings, so I was crying. My uncle, who was my mother's eldest brother and who subsequently adopted me and became my dad, came in and said to my grandmother, "Tell you what, get her dressed and I'll bring her over to Frank and Jill [his son and daughter]".

So my [adoptive] dad brought me down to his house. I always remember going in and Frank and Jill were there. It wasn't my first time to see them, of course, but he brought me in and here they were, and Jill said to her father, "Can we keep her?" like I was a little doll. I stayed that night, and eventually my bags came over from my granny's house. My adoptive mother was amazing and she absolutely adored me. Growing up, you don't think any different. It's only when you have your own children or maybe when I look at, say, my sister-in-law's children, and I'm thinking, *Could I love them the way my mother loved me?*

I was completely loved be everyone, not just in my own family but by all my uncles and aunts. I was put into everything: ballroom dancing, tap dancing and ballet. When I was young, I was a real novelty as well, and I know that all the family were very proud of me and took an interest in me. In so many ways, it was far better than being adopted by strangers. I was eight years old when I was formally adopted. I remember being in the adoption agency and having a balloon. I left go of the string, and it flew up and stuck to the ceiling, which was very high, and somebody had to get a ladder and take it down. And I remember that the room was full of people, and my mother and father had to place their hands on the Bible as though they were in court.

We lived first near my granny's in a flat in Benburb Street. I made my communion when we still lived in Benburb Street and went to school in George's Hill. My granny used to work in the market, and at one time she had a pitch on the Ha'penny Bridge and used to sell little chickens in wicker baskets. She was a widow and an amazing woman.

Then we got a house in Cabra. Many of my aunts had moved out to Cabra by that time, and that's where I grew up and made friends.

Cabra wasn't a bad place to grow up. I don't know about growing up different from everyone else, because obviously you are, but I never thought that I was. You don't realise you are different until you look in the mirror. In my mind, I was always "Lisa the dancer" — tap dancing and ballroom dancing. Even when people see me now — older women especially if I see them in town or if they come into the shop where I work — they will say things like, "There is Lisa. Lisa the dancer."

I have to say I was never badly treated. Ever. When I look back now, my mother was the youngest of a family of seven, and when she had me I was totally loved by all her family. I mean, my communion day was a big event for all the family, even though most of them had children of their own. One of my cousins even had her communion in the same month as me, but somehow it was always about Lisa.

Growing up as the centre of attention
When I was very young, my [natural] mother had a friend who was from Ghana. He and his wife had two children, and they came and stayed on two occasions in my aunt's

house. Otherwise I never met anyone like that. Going back to the sixties, you were always surrounded by white people, and you'd never see any black people except on TV. I think the mid-teen years of fourteen and fifteen were an awkward time for me. Maybe you'd be going down the road with a friend and see a group of boys, and then you didn't want to walk down that way because you knew they were going to jeer you or say something to you. Things like "nig nog" or silly little things like that. My friend would tell them to shut up, but I'd prefer if she didn't even speak to them because that made it worse. I don't think kids do this nowadays, but when I was young there was no political correctness. There were even programmes on TV like "Love Thy Neighbour", with a black family and a white family living next door to one another. They'd jeer each other all the time, and the names used in these kinds of programmes were the ones the boys on the street would call you. In those days it was plastered all over the TV, even with things like the gollywog on the marmalade jars, and people would call you "gollywog". And then, when you were a year or two older, there was an awakening because you had grown into a woman, and then they looked at you differently and wanted to take you out — those same fellas!

But my family were always so supportive, and I couldn't say that I felt any different to any of my cousins or any of my family. Maybe when I look back now my memories would be of dancing, and people might be saying, "Look at the lovely dress and the colour of her!" But it was grand. Sometimes you'd feel a bit left out, but kids aren't really racist. You'd start in a new school and kids wouldn't treat you any differently, girls don't anyway, and you all grow up together.

I think that me being brought up in the family was a bonus for my [natural] mother because she knew at every stage how I was getting on. When I was a teenager and going out at night, my [adoptive] mother and father used to always say, "You'd better be back at such a time, because if anything happens to you, Angela will have our guts for garters." That's what I had to listen to all through the years. Even though they had legally adopted me, they were still afraid that if anything happened they would be accountable to her.

Anyway, I went to secondary school in town. Growing up in the seventies, we all wanted to get the bus into town and to go to school there, so a few of us went to school in Parnell Square. I still have contact with some of those girls that I went to school with. Unfortunately, and I could kick myself now, I only did two years in school. I couldn't wait to leave and get a job, although I was actually fairly good in school. I had just sat my Group Cert. My family didn't really encourage me to stay on because they were workers themselves. Probably the attitude at the time was that girls would get married anyway. I was fifteen when I left school, and it was the norm at the time for working-class families like us.

Marriage and family

I was working in the summer following my Group Cert; then September came round, and I didn't go back to school. When I was in school, I'd ask permission to go out on a Saturday night, and they'd say, "No." But if I left school and was working, I'd be allowed out once a week into town, which is where we went for our entertainment at the time. I thought it was great to get out once a week. A whole load of us left school at the same time. It wasn't much of a job, but soon afterwards my cousin got me a job in the place where she worked. I moved there and stayed for two years until I left to get married.

We were very young, both of us, and people wouldn't do it now, but it worked for us. We are still together and still love one another. He was only eighteen. My first child, James, was born, and I had three children by the time I was twenty-one. It didn't do me any harm, but I wouldn't wish it for my own children.

My husband lived in Ballyfermot, so when we married we lived in his mother's house for four years or so. I didn't really know people in the area, but I got to know people. I took to Ballyfermot really well and found the people very nice. After a while we got our own house, and all our kids have been brought up there. I'm very easy to get on with. My husband's sister used to come up every day and she was a kind of friend to me, and every day I'd go up and down to the shops. When you think back on it, that is all we had at the time. I'm no good for moving. My husband, John, is a bricklayer, and years ago he used to talk about moving away. He even suggested that we move to the country, but that wouldn't suit me at all. I like to feel that there are people around and things going on, even though I mightn't see anyone from one end of the day to the other.

I find that I'm more or less known in my own area, so I don't generally get asked about my colour. A few years ago, that used to happen more often. Now I'm always in familiar situations where people know me. In the past, people might say, "Where were you born?" and I'd say, "Well, I was born in London, my mother was Irish and my father from Ghana." They don't usually ask me anything else after that. Sometimes when I speak to people that don't know me, as soon as I open my mouth I can see them warming to me because I don't have a different accent as though I was from a different country. It seems to reassure people and break down barriers.

As regards my children, people are more curious because they can't put their finger on their origins. Sometimes I wonder how it is for my kids, growing up. James, the eldest, is quite dark. He is sallow skinned, but, in a manner of speaking, he has grown up into a black man. When he was younger, he looked Spanish or Italian, but then his hair grew tighter. People use to call him "Will Smith" at the time. He has a lovely personality. At times I worry about him meeting people. Not girlfriends, because young people are open-minded, but their families. He's going out with a girl now for three years, and very early on her mother came over and introduced herself to me, which was very nice. But you still worry about them, because you do get bad-minded people. Then again, maybe it's that they just want their kids to be happy and they don't want them to have extra trouble in their lives. You can't blame them for that. I mean, if my daughter came in tomorrow and said she was going to marry someone who was black, it would be no problem to me, but if the person was from Africa — well, the colour wouldn't be a problem, but I'd worry about the difference in their cultures. Many people are amazed that me and John are together for twenty-one years, but that has nothing to do with colour.

Blood and other relatives

My [natural] mother used to come back to Dublin every so often, and then eventually she returned for good and settled down and got married. She must have been in her thirties by that time. I'm glad really that she found somebody and married. Sometimes I think that, had she kept me, it would have been harder for her to get married. Realistically I was glad the way the situation worked out. She seemed happy enough. I suppose I don't really know very much about her life because I didn't really know her that well. I have a half-brother and two half-sisters. They knew when they were growing up that I was their mother's child. They certainly weren't kept in the dark about me. My [natural] mother was very open about me. I recall an incident that happened when Angela's youngest child was born. I went to see Angela in the hospital, and her older daughter said, "I've got two sisters now and one brother."

I always remember when Jake, her eldest, was born I wasn't very pleased. I did love her, not as a mother, but I remember thinking at the time, *God, she's my mother and she's after having a baby.* And yet I didn't want to be with her and I preferred the family I was in. I was lucky to have what I had, but I had mixed feelings about it as well.

I think I felt quite bitter towards her when I had my own child. When James was born, I thought, *My God, how could she have given her child away?* I was only seventeen at the time, and later, when I got older, I realised that she did what she had to do.

I never talked to Angela about myself. I didn't want to hurt her. When I was growing up, if I was out and happened to see my mother, I could see that she was always very proud of me, but I'd be saying to myself, *If I'd been with her, God knows how I'd have ended up.* I know I shouldn't have felt like that, but I was young at the time and had less understanding. In a way, I think I was punishing her. I didn't know, of course, that she was going to die so young. Nowadays I'm driving and I've much more time to myself. If Angela were alive today, I'd certainly go over and visit her more, but at that time I had young kids. I was more tied down and it was different. Then they both [natural and adoptive mothers] died, almost together: Angela in February and my [adoptive] mother in April 1981 and my [adoptive] father the following year. My [adoptive] mother was probably in her forties when I was adopted, so she was quite a bit older than Angela, about sixty-nine. But Angela was just fifty-four years old when she died. I took the death of my adoptive mother harder because I was closer to her. It was the same for my children, because she was the only grandmother that they knew.

When I used to mention Angela to my adoptive mother, she'd get a small bit jealous. She was sick by that time, and we knew she was going to die. I said to myself, *If anything happens to my mother, I'll probably end up going more to Angela.* I meant visiting her or just seeing a bit more of her. Then Angela died first, and I thought, *Did God do this to me as a way of telling me that I can't have my cake and eat it.* It was very strange.

I thought of Angela as an aunt. When she was sick, I rushed to the hospital and we formed a vigil around her bed. I know she was delighted about that. After that she recovered, and it was two years later when she died. I don't think anybody expected her to die at that time because she was quite young. My reaction to her death was strange as well. I got a phone call from my cousin telling me that she was dead. They were all in the hospital, and I asked my cousin, "What do you want me to do? Will I come over to the hospital?" but my cousin said that there was no point in going there then but to wait until the following day. I had to collect Andrea [daughter], but I didn't really need to do that. Somebody else could have collected her for me. Later I found out that they were all down in the hospital waiting for me to arrive. When I went to the funeral parlour, people kept coming up to me saying, "I'm very sorry to hear about your mother," and it was so strange. At that time my [adoptive] mother was still alive, of course, but she had had a number of strokes and was quite ill. It was all very strange to me.

I never told my children that Angela was their grandmother, and they really didn't see her very often. It was sad in ways. With hindsight, maybe I denied her the children. I don't think I did it deliberately, but it was confusing enough for me growing up, and I wanted things to be as normal as possible, so they didn't really know my mother. With the children, I try to have things as stable as possible and to have no complications. Maybe when my kids grow up and have children of their own, if they didn't bring them to see me, I would probably feel left out like my mother might have felt. I'm not sure.

Angela had three other children — two girls and a boy. The boy, Jake, is the eldest and is nine years younger than me. Her youngest daughter is the same age as my eldest son. When Angela died, Jake clung to me a bit. I'm not quite sure why. When he met my kids, I introduced him as their uncle, and he seemed pleased. He asked if it would be OK if he visited. I assured him that my door was always open for him, so Jake started to come and visit us regularly, about once a week. I don't see the girls as often. Jake had a job that took him away for long periods so I saw him less. Their father is still at home, and I always felt that in ways I was a thorn in his side, being his wife's first child whom she talked about all the time. I don't tend to go and visit. I'll drop out sometime, but I don't like to invade their space. Maybe I'm just leaving things go, yet I know I shouldn't do that. I should learn from the mistakes of the past.

I hadn't seen Jake for a long time, and just yesterday he turned up on my door and has a small son now. It was the first time I ever saw his child, and I didn't know if he had said to him, "This is your aunt," or what, but I was looking at him thinking, *I'm his aunt* — my flesh and blood. It's nice, this connection. When you are a different colour, it's harder to see resemblances with relatives. People do say that I resemble one or two of my cousins, but it is very nice for me, all these connections when you are used to being on your own. I'm always in contact with my [adoptive] brother and sister. We go out occasionally with Frank. Now and again if he comes over to us and we go out together, somebody who hasn't met him before will ask, "Who's he?" and John would always say, "That's Lisa's brother." In so many ways, I was never separated from my family.

My father is the only part of my life that I know nothing about. A few years ago, Jake was saying to me, "You probably have brothers and sisters that are more like you. You'd probably feel more towards them." I don't think I would, not simply because of colour. I may never get to know about my father because I tend to be laid back about looking. I think I'd just like to say, "Hello," to have a look and then go. We'd probably keep in contact, but in some ways I don't know what I would be letting myself in for. I have a birth cert. But his name is not on it, just my mother's name. I think about looking for him and finding him all the time. One or two of my aunts probably know a bit more about him. It's not that they are keeping information from me, but I just never asked. And yet it's silly to wait too long and never to speak about it, because when people are dead it's too late. If my [natural] mother were alive, she would be about sixty and he would be getting older as well.

I never spoke to Angela about him. She did tell me a few stories when I was growing up, but I'm not sure if she made them up. When I was younger, I remember her writing a letter to this man called Alex. She said he was from Ghana. She'd write the letter and then I'd copy it out in my writing. I mentioned earlier that my mother had a friend who was Ghanaian who came to stay in my aunt's house with his family. Obviously my mother mixed in those circles in London. That man is a doctor now. One of my cousins thought at the time that he was my father, but he isn't. She suggested that if I contacted him, and I know his name and the hospital that he is attached to, he might be able to help me find my father. I've always wondered about my father. You never get anywhere just wondering, but I'm a very relaxed person. I should look for him. My husband thinks I'm mad. He says, if it was him, he'd just do it.

In a way I'd be afraid of opening up a can of worms. Maybe I'm afraid of rejection. As well as that, I have such an extended family, and I'm not sure if I'm ready for any more. But I'd love to meet him and look at him. I don't look like my mother and I haven't got her characteristics. I tend to be very soft hearted, and my mother was quite sharp. I wonder if I have his temperament. You do like to know where you come from. When you have your own children, you have things like vaccinations and you are asked about medical history, and you have to say, "I don't know." My little boy was saying the other day that if he was a footballer he could play for three countries, and I asked him how that was, and he said, "Well, Nanny was born in Ireland, you were born in London and wasn't my real granddad born in Ghana?"

And yet, when I think about it, I know a few black people, but they are all half-Irish. I don't really know anybody from Africa. Sometimes I ask myself, would it be strange speaking to somebody from Africa? That sounds silly, I know, but it's true because it's such a different world.

Sometimes I'm a bit disappointed that he never came looking for me. It would have been easier for him than it is for me. He obviously knew the name that my mother gave me. She called me Alicia. It would be nice to know where you come from. I know I was loved by my family and that was all I needed, but when your parent is a different colour, it's nice to meet them and to try and relate to them.

If I sat down and dwelt on everything, I'd probably crack up, but I was very young getting married, and I had my kids while I was still very young, so I never had the chance to sit down and brood. Having family around, you just pick yourself up and get on with things. It's only when you talk about it that you realise how sad it all is. I realise that life is far too short for bitterness. My natural mother and I never fought, but I never really got close to her either. I was never badly treated, but your feelings are hurt because of being given up. I still can't help feeling a bit hurt about that, although I do understand.

It's different for black men

It's different for men and women. I really think it's harder for men. Do you know that black men are the most dying race of people in the world? It was actually a quiz question — what is the fastest dying race of people? It's probably mainly due to violence. We have a friend, Derek, who's half-Irish and half-Trinadadian. He looks younger than his years, and if we are all out together he is sometimes mistaken for my son. He gets a great kick out of that. Or people might ask if we are brother and sister. I always have great patience with people. I mean, if I saw two Chinese people sitting together, I'd probably ask them if they were brother and sister. But Derek gets jibes from blokes for being with white women, which he only ever is, of course. It's the same with me — I married a white man. I wasn't in a position to marry somebody of my own colour. Derek gets hassled over that, but they would never say anything to my husband for being with me. It's totally different for me. If my husband is with me, people are not going to say, "He's with a black woman." Maybe I was always shielded by my husband, but I think it was easier for me.

Things are harder for men anyway but are harder still for black men, and that is why I fear for my son. He is quite dark, especially when he has been in the sun, and he works outside with his father. He is the only one of the family with jet-black hair. He is a good-looking boy, people often admire him and he is well-liked. But I still fear for him.

69

What about the children?

My younger daughter is obsessed with black people. Really obsessed. She watches them on the TV or wherever she sees them, and she wants to marry a black man and have black children. I said to her that, if she does, then I won't die out altogether.

I asked a friend how he would define my son, James, and he said without stopping to think, "A black man." It's so strange because they are my kids and I don't think of them in terms of colour. I said, "All right, how would you describe Diana [eldest daughter] then?"

He hesitated and said, "I couldn't." He felt that he couldn't call her a black woman because if you look at her you don't see that. They are brother and sister from the same mother and father, and yet you could say one is black and one isn't. I still didn't feel James should be categorised as a black man. I said it to James when he came home, and he just said, "I wish I was."

Other people's reactions

People don't mean to be offensive or bad. We are all ignorant in ways. I mean, if I see black people walking down the road, I'll be staring at them. I'm amazed at the tone of their skin and the reddish glow off some people. I find it beautiful. Sometimes people, whom I think are refugees, come into the shop. They don't necessarily come to my counter, but if they do I always smile and try to make some contact with them. Some of them don't seem to be very friendly, but I think it's because some, the women in particular, are quite fearful. I think probably people know from looking at you whether you are a stranger or not. Obviously when people hear you speak, they'd know you are from Ireland.

I suppose I try and look at everyone's point of view. If I was talking to somebody all evening and then, at the end of the evening, he introduced me to his wife and she was Chinese, I know I would get a tiny bit of a shock. It's because you presume the person is white, and then if it turns out that they are not. . . For example, I've often spoken on the phone to people, and later if they meet me in person, I notice that they always show some reaction, however slight.

You try to protect your family from this a bit. I often wondered if Jake might be, not quite ashamed, but maybe embarrassed. I remember we were out one night some years ago at a karaoke session. We were sitting beside this man who knows John and myself. Jake was with us, and when he went up to sing, this man asked, "Who is that?"

Somebody said, "It's Lisa's brother," and he said, "Oh, yea? He's just like her as well!" Now I'm not a forward kind of person, but John told me what he said, and I did go over to him, and I said, "Excuse me, but he is my brother. We come from the same mother. Would that class us as brother and sister or what?" But I know that people can't help it.

Is it because of colour?

As I said, I probably had it easier than many people. I'm not saying I could hide behind my husband, but he has always been there, so my colour has never been an issue that I've had to deal with. Maybe when I'm not around, he has had to deal with it. I don't know. But we do talk about it. Earlier we were talking about me coming to see you, and John was saying that because I don't experience racism I don't need to get involved. But that is wrong. It's like saying, "If it's not on our doorstep, we can ignore it."

James said, "If my ma can give an interview that can help, then it's good."

It's funny, I was saying that I don't experience it [racism] and now it's all coming back to me. There was an incident that comes to mind. I was driving a couple of months ago and there were four cars in front of mine, all indicating to turn left. This man came out of the pub and he was obviously drunk, and he reversed into two of the cars, pushing the car in front into mine. My car wasn't too badly damaged, although later we found it amounted to £1,000 worth of damages. The police arrived after a while, and it was clear that the three cars in front of me were in bits. Mine didn't look too bad. One of the policemen said, "What are you waiting for? Stand over there until I'm ready for you."

Anyway, when they had interviewed everyone else, he came over and said, "Is this your car?" I said that it was. Then he asked me where I lived, and I said in Cherry Orchard. Now Cherry Orchard has a bad name, but where I live is fine. Then he asked me my name, and when I told him, he asked, "Are you any relation of X?" And I said, "No. I've never been involved with the police in my life."

He seemed very suspicious. I don't know if it was my colour or because I lived in Cherry Orchard. I could get paranoid about it, and I don't want to. If you did, life wouldn't be worth living.

I was saying it to my husband, and he thought it was disgraceful. He said he'd complain about it because he had to go down to the police station anyway. When he went down, he said to the policeman who was there, "I wasn't very pleased with the way my wife was treated." The policeman said the man concerned was out and would be in later. My husband just left it because you never get the better of them in the end. He just said to me, "If this is what happened to you, what is going to happen to James?" And it's a worry.

My husband and I do talk about it, but not all the time. I often wonder if, when he's meeting people for the first time, he explains to them that I'm black. Sometimes I wish he would because it gives people a chance to get over their reaction, and people always do show a reaction of surprise, no matter how slight. It probably wouldn't be obvious to other people.

A case of mistaken identity and defining the self

I know that there are a few black people that grew up in Ballyfermot, and it's funny because I still get called by their names. There was a woman called Stella, and when I go into the cleaners the girl there, for no particular reason, always writes "Stella" on my ticket. Then a lot of people think I am the woman who has the hairdresser's shop. Actually they think I am her so much that my husband was stopped once and accused of having an affair. All over a case of mistaken identity. Just a couple of weeks ago, a person came into the shop and said to me, "Are you still at the hairdressing?"

I said straight out, "It's not me. I was never hairdressing."

She said, "Are you sure about that?"

It just like you are black and they don't see beyond that. She said then, "Are you sure, because I'm great with faces?" She was a bit narked about it, even as much as to say, "You all look the same."

Now, I use the word black to describe myself, but I didn't always. When I was growing up, you were "coloured", but then all of a sudden that word is not being used any more. I used to never like being regarded as "black", or being "coloured" either for that matter, but somehow, these days, it seems to be the norm.

Jude

ANYWAY, ALL THAT HAS NOTHING TO DO WITH COLOUR, HAS IT?

Jude grew up in an industrial school in Kerry. As an adolescent, he moved to Dublin and settled down as an apprentice tailor. He built up a steady business and in later years began making trips to African countries.

At the time of the interview, he and his wife, who is Zambian, were expecting their first child. Jude felt that he was more aware than before of having no known living relative and that this was becoming more of an issue for him with the impending birth of his child.

The child

Because you are coloured, everyone makes a fuss of you. It's like being a novelty. You get thrown by that, and you think everybody loves black people. This is a falseness that hits you, eventually, when you grow up. When you grow up, it's not like you thought it was. That is when the shock comes. I reckon I didn't notice until I was thirteen or fourteen. Up to that, I thought I was popular. You'd be picked for teams because somebody would say, "Black people are great at sports," and you were thrown into playing music because you are supposed to be good at music. And you are dumped into a band. You get a chance of learning music and reading music and playing music, but somebody put you there because somebody said, "Black people are great at music." It has advantages, but afterwards you realise how stupid that was. I got on reasonably well in sports, but I didn't want to go any further as it was only meant to be for recreation.

I remember the troubles in America over civil rights, also something about South Africa, and I questioned why people were against black people. Then I read more and more and I got information from people. I found out that there were actually laws against people walking into restaurants, that there were white areas and black areas. I couldn't believe it really, the hatred and the violence that all those issues caused and that it could go on anywhere if it went on there.

Usually there was a bit of news on the radio, and you would question a bit more about why it was happening. I couldn't understand it because of the myth that everybody loved black people. That suddenly got shattered, and the reality was that it wasn't exactly like that. While you were cosy and comfortable and well protected in Ireland, it was not exactly that way at all.

I didn't know any other black people. At times I thought I was the only black person in Ireland. In school, I was the only black person, and maybe because of that I stood out. I was taken notice of. That in itself caused problems. Being black was still a novelty down the country. You knew that when you went out to the shops. They don't mean it, it's just that they are not used to it, especially when you go to far-out places.

OK, there are a few people, coloured people, in the shops in towns in Kerry now, but back then to see a coloured person in those places was rare. I could never understand when they would ask me where I was from and I'd say I was born in Dublin, and then they'd say, "But no, where are you really from?"

That kind of thing. Now that got so repetitive I got fed up with it.

The institution
I was first in Stillorgan, St Philomena's. Then I got

transferred to a place in Dún Laoghaire. That was closed and I got transferred for four or five years to a place in Tralee called St Joseph's Industrial School. Carriglee [Dún Laoghaire] and St Joseph's were both Christian Brothers and St Philomena's was Sisters of Charity.

I learnt a trade in Tralee. In fact, Tralee was the best place I was in. The activities were better there. Workwise and music-wise, a hell of a lot of things were better. That was up to sixteen years old. But there were two areas that I thought were very bad. You had a person, let's say where one of their parents died, who got shoved into these places. The others, who were criminals, got shoved in with them. Those who had no parents, orphans, people like me, were brought up in institutions. They were thrown in on the same level as those kids who were sent there by the courts, and that was appalling. As far as the Christian Brothers were concerned, everyone in the place was a criminal. I don't know who allowed this to happen, and I'm glad the Kennedy Report found that it was wrong. Those kids should have been adopted or fostered. A lot of them were dumped out into farms and worked like slaves. Some of them slept in barns and were not allowed into the house. I met some of these people in the school, and some of their stories were frightening.

I'm amazed how I came through it. It does have an effect because it does hold you back and you are afraid to do things. You aren't sure of yourself sometimes. You are afraid of the consequences, especially when you are completely on your own. In the home, the children were all different. Some were able to go home once a month, and you could see the difference in the boys who went out. They might go home for the summer holidays and you would never go, and you would be aware that it was different for them.

But overall in Tralee, I found it nice. Some of the people down there took an interest in me, and I ended up going off some Sundays with them and spending holidays with them. That was one of the main reasons why I liked Tralee. It was a bit more liberal than a lot of places; there was more freedom. Down there, I played trumpet with the band and I marched around with some of the famous Kerry teams. It was a band like the Artane Boys' Band. I knew Mick O'Connell and O'Dwyer when they would be marching in their team behind the band. Little did I know that they would become so famous as footballers. Later on, when I moved up to Dublin, I joined a band, but I dropped that as I was too involved. It was hectic when I left school. I was in a basketball club, the band and then I was in An Óige and I belonged to the Heinkel Scooter Club of Ireland. I reckon all my activities kept me sane when I left.

I think everybody in those places could write a book. I mean, a lot of the time you put up with things because they were the norm. There were appalling cruelties in these places, and afterwards you thought, *Why did I put up with that?* I had a fight with this brother over eating my dinner. I wouldn't eat it, and he left it on the table and said, "Kneel at the back there until you are ready to eat it." An hour later I was still kneeling on the floor, and he was prepared to leave me kneeling for hours if he had to. So I got up, picked up the dinner, went up to him and threw the whole plate at him. To my amazement, he did nothing. I was like a hero in the school after that.

There were some brothers who were brilliant and some who were the opposite. That was the problem. The good ones were very good. A few of them really helped me. One or two of them said they would really love to get me into secondary school; they had the attitude that I had a reasonable brain. But some only became brothers to please their mothers. They hadn't the vocation. You could see the ones who had, the difference between them. You had some who only wanted to have authority as it gave them a sadistic kick. Others wouldn't hurt a fly. They stood out. The gas part of it was that they were the ones who always won in the end. They were always the more respected. It showed that they didn't need all the bullying. Some of them thought that by beating you they would get your respect, but like the old saying, you have to earn it, and some of them certainly earned it the right way. And others — well, you couldn't respect them. Bullying didn't win them respect.

Leaving the institution

There is a problem when you leave a secure place. Suddenly you are out in the wide world. I found that it was disastrous for a lot of people brought up in institutions. Some people came through it and others couldn't handle it. I think it was worse for the girls. A lot of them had a new-found freedom. It looks terrific. You are able to go to the cinema any time you want. You can go to any restaurant and buy anything you want. You are aged sixteen, earning money, and you think the world is at your feet. Some people spend, spend, spend, and they forget that they have to pay for things, too. They are in rented accommodation, and between this and the fact that they are used to being with crowds of people and suddenly they are on their own, the loneliness gets to them. They have no friends. But that could happen whether you are coloured or white; it has nothing to do with being coloured.

There is a danger that you'll fall back, and you don't want to be running back to the school. So there was that pressure, and it was a hell of a lot of pressure to put on people, to succeed; and what happened to a lot of people is that they had to put up with being treated badly and that did terrible psychological damage. It either makes you or breaks you, and when you think of the consequences, that is enough to keep you going. I know one girl, and ever since she left the protection of the home she has not been able to do anything. She used to go back, even up to recently, to this nun she used to know as a kid, but now this nun is eighty-something and she can't help her any longer. This person is now in a psychiatric hospital and she has never been able to cope, but nothing was done when she left the home. She should have been helped and supported.

There are an awful lot of lies about the past. Today people are more honest. People then lived a lie. The situation for children born out of marriage was even worse back then; they hid it. Rich people got their kids dumped into places, and they were just forgotten about. Those people, some of them, never found out about their background, and they were never allowed to think out about who they were. It left an appalling legacy of hitting a brick wall and getting no further. Now the laws have changed, but they could still get away with it back then. The Church covered up a lot of it. I think a lot of damage was done, and it was very unfair to these people.

I don't know where I got this thing of "Don't sit around doing nothing," but I found myself going like the hammers of hell. In fact, sometimes I was trying to fit two or three events together — playing in the band, basketball, weekends away with the Heinkel Club. It was crazy. I was in An Óige, cycling down to Kilkenny on the bike. I was going to the tech at night, in Parnell Square. Anyway, all that has nothing to do with colour, has it?

Working life

After I left I was sent tailoring up here in Lower Abbey Street. I stayed in the Catholic Boys' Home. It used to be here, in Middle Abbey Street, and then it moved to Eccles Street, but I had moved out by that time. When you are in an institution, you are not given much choice. I mean, some people asked me how I ended up with tailoring, and I said, "Look, you are in an industrial school. You learn trades. You don't go to secondary school. You do your primary and then you are dumped into a trade. They had carpentry, shoemaking and tailoring, and it was a question of which one of them do you want to be."

Looking at the people working at carpentry and the people doing shoemaking, I saw more accidents happening to them, so I picked tailoring. People had got their hands cut with saws, and then you had others who were black with all the polish and wax, and sometimes they would break their fingers hammering their fingers rather than the shoes; you saw all of this while you were at school, so, of course, you'd say to yourself, *I'll make sure I won't go into that trade.* So, really, I just took the soft option and went for the safest. I suppose, with hindsight, if I got the choice I would gladly have gone to secondary school, but that option wasn't there. It didn't arise in those places.

Apprenticeships really whittled out in my time. The old way was you had to do your seven years, but that all went. As far as most people were concerned, if you could work and make a suit or make anything, they'd employ you because you could do the job. It didn't matter if you had a certificate. I did do City and Guilds at the tech at intermediate level, but I didn't go any further because the tailors would say to me, "Look, we don't read papers. We only want to see if you can make a suit or make trousers or a pocket." You could learn it all in theory but not be able to do it in practice.

So I stayed at it. I was on my own and I had no choice. I had to survive. A lot of things you don't have a choice about when you are dumped out in the world like that and told that you have to survive. Who would have supported me? I learnt in other ways by travel and reading about situations all over the world, and I took a terrific interest in that. So as far as I was concerned, that became my education.

I started up on my own in the tailoring in 1978. I was in Ormond Quay then and I was doing terrific. I used to specialise in making trousers. Everyone used to get suits made around Christmas time back in those days. Even by September you would be booked up to Christmas. But ready-made clothes came in and slowly wiped out the tailoring by, I reckon, 70 per cent. I would say that only about 20 or 30 per cent of the hand-crafted tailors are left in Dublin. When this happened, I found myself in trouble. Then it opened up a new era, because when people started buying ready-mades, it left a big opening in alterations, but I had to be more central. Ormond Quay was out of the way for repairs. Out of the blue, I got an offer of a place on Middle Abbey Street in 1986. It was perfect, and the rest is history.

Racism

I tell you that psychological damage can be done to people even in, let's say, mixed marriages, depending on the treatment the kids get from other people. When the kids turn up at school, that is the start of the problems. They are made to feel that there is something wrong with them, that they are inadequate, and it is very hurtful. They are used to the protection and care of a mother, but now they have to face new people. If anything goes wrong, if they do anything against another person, they are insulted immediately. They are told, "You black bastard, go back to where you came from," even though they are born in Ireland. These kind of things happen. People pass remarks because of the ignorance of the culture from where they come, and the kids have to put up with a lot of this. It affects some people. They wonder, "Why do we have to put up with this?" They even wish they were white. That to me is very serious, that they get to a stage where they are rejecting their own culture. I found that it certainly has effects like that.

At the moment, race involves such a small minority that people don't take much notice. They are not a threat. The day they become a threat is when all this will change. The idea is to stop it before that day comes. The number of people is getting bigger and bigger. There is a terribly big mixed-race population already in Dublin. I'm amazed to find how big it is. I'm married to a Zambian girl, and practically ever since she has come on the scene, I'm amazed at the amount of people who have gone abroad teaching and engineering and come back with African wives. There are a huge amount married to Zambians, Tanzanians, South Africans, and all living here. I never realised how big a number it was until I started meeting them at get-togethers. Because I married a Zambian girl, we know four or five Zambian girls living here that I wouldn't come across otherwise.

Strategies for dealing with racism

It would be a good idea to speak to other mixed-race people about it [racism], especially when they are kids. The way I came through it was by being involved in sports and the other activities. That helps to break down barriers, and then they don't see you for your colour — they see you as a person. It is important that the other kids around you see you for who you are. If they just keep seeing your colour, there is something wrong. It has got to be broken down with a group of friends, a group of people that you live with, that you go to school with. It would be great, having done that, if they stand by you, because they would stick by you in times of trouble. That helps. But if it doesn't work like that for those kids who have started school and get bad vibes already, quite the opposite will happen. They won't mix, and they will find it hard, after-wards, to trust other white people because of that experience. So, it is very important for the mixed kid to feel he or she belongs, to make that effort to break that barrier. Naturally no kid will ever understand why he has to do that, but I think that it is an area that mothers and fathers should seriously consider: getting the child to develop real friendships with friends who will stand by them and help them, because sometimes the damage that gets done can get worse and worse. I'd love if people who are dealing with mixed-race children got together and talked about these problems. I mean, some of the stories I have heard are appalling. Anybody who thinks these things don't happen . . ., but they do happen, and the psychological damage that is done to these kids is terrible.

I still have friends from my time in Tralee. Even when I got married, my best man was somebody I knew from Tralee. He is a detective now. There are one or two others who were at my wedding that go back to schooldays. The contact was always there. There are four of us who are permanent friends. They are scattered all over the world now, but we still keep in contact.

Searching for roots

I only got this letter the other day. I have been trying for ten years to find out more information about myself. This is about the third letter I have got, and at last somebody has asked me to contact them, almost when I have given up hope. I find that appalling, but they might surprise me yet.

They are all closed down now, but I never went back to the homes. I was getting nowhere. I was told to check with the homes, and I was told where I was born and no more, and I wasn't taken seriously. Now they seem to be moving, but you'd nearly have to have a row with them before they move. As far as I'm concerned, it should be a legal right. The Eastern Health Board have the records, I know that much. Those records were all passed on when the homes closed down.

Part of my problem is not knowing. I never took that seriously before because I was too busy trying to get on with my own life, but I find as you get on in years, and particularly if you get married and have a family, you need to be able to tell your kid who you are and where you come from. I wouldn't be able to give much background information about myself, so maybe I am lucky that this letter has appeared out of the blue. The timing is good. I'm sick of not being able to explain my background, and I get sick of the way it is purposefully hidden. I know stories of people who made the effort and did get somewhere, but some of it was disastrous. In some cases, people suddenly appeared on the door-step when they should have used the social worker. I mean, maybe this social worker, who has written to me, can be a kind of go-between. That is the way I am going to approach it. You don't want to crash in, especially if they are in another marriage or something like that. I would respect their privacy because you have to remember that circumstances could have driven them into that. People were treated badly if they had a child out of marriage. Some of them were banned from their houses. Some of them were almost kicked out of the country. It was appalling.

So I understand their side of the situation. This is, maybe, a hidden background. I wouldn't blame them for that because in those days that is the way things were done. People go on about how things have got out of hand today, but now things are far better. There is far more honesty. People know who they are and where they come from. There is none of this "Get them into institutions and forget about them." But there is a gap with people going back to the fifties, the forties and even the thirties. People were just left stranded. Before this I started looking a few times for my mother, but I certainly don't think you should get completely besotted by it. Some people do. I will do it, but I will get on with the rest of my life as well. I have the attitude that I have managed so far and nobody has come looking for me, so all I want is background information. That is all. Except that I might get a surprise.

Identity and others' perceptions

Sometimes I don't notice my colour, but then, other times, I'm made aware of it. It would be nice to be able to carry on, and sometimes I can get by with ignoring it, but at the same time you have to face reality and the fact that some people do see your colour. When I am dealing with customers, once they know you, there is no problem. They are terrific. Others walk in here, particularly the new ones, and they will come thundering down the stairs, and sometimes they will say to me, "Oh, can I see the boss?" If I want to be funny, I'll put the other fella on to them and say, "John [Jude's assistant], they want to speak to you." But I'm having a big laugh. Then there are others who walk in and when they see me they will say, "I think I'm in the wrong place." You can see them with the bag of stuff they have brought along. Some of them don't know how to handle the situation. They have to learn how to deal with you as a black person. That is a problem. Well, it isn't a problem for me; it is their problem. As far as I'm concerned, I don't have a problem in dealing with anyone. In fact, in meeting customers I come across all types and walks of life from the highest to the lowest. They are all different and you learn how to deal with them all.

There were problems with sport and other things for me in Tralee, especially with boxing. I remember hearing about Joe Louis and Floyd Patterson back then, and I would be delighted if they won their fights. The problem was, people would say to me, "You think you are great. Who do you think you are, Floyd Patterson?"

Sometimes I'd have to fight — not because I'm Jude Hughes, but because they would decide I was Floyd Patterson. Whether I liked it or not, they would decide to fight me. Sometimes I came out the worst. Looking back on it now, I wonder why I did take that kind of nonsense. But every kid thinks that they are this person or that person. Sometimes it was a matter of honour. And, sometimes, you would do it out of pure pride because you felt you couldn't let the side down.

I have been to Africa — to Tanzania. When I went, I didn't go like a tourist. I ended up having tremendous conversations with people I met. I remember I was in the Dar es Salaam museum and I got chatting to someone there, and he put me in touch with somebody else who gave me a whole load of African poetry. He put on an evening for the whole group that I was with. It was a great session.

I feel it is a good thing for black people to go to Africa, because it is like going back to old roots. You might not have any connection with Tanzania or whichever country you go to, but you realise that all the black people in America or the Caribbean all were from that part of the world. That is good to see as it gives you a feeling of a different kind of belonging.

Luzveminda

OVERALL, I HAD AN ORDINARY KIND OF CHILDHOOD . . .

Luzveminda O'Sullivan, a post-graduate student of Trinity College, was crowned Rose of Tralee in August 1998. During her reign, she agreed to launch Trócaire's campaign for Africa, "Sudan Needs Change", and made Trócaire her official charity for the year.

Her commitment to the organisation for the duration of her reign was reinforced by Trócaire's long track record of working in the Philippines. The fact that her mother, who died tragically when Luzveminda was a child, was from the Philippines made this a special connection for her.

Childhood

When I was born in the county hospital, we lived in a place called Glenisland, about eight miles outside of Castlebar. My mum was from the Philippines and my dad comes from a place called Knockmore, just outside of Ballina.

I was the first of five. We are all very close in age in our family. I'm twenty-four now, my sister who is next to me is twenty-three and the others are twenty-one, nineteen and eighteen. So growing up, myself and my sister socialised together. We went to the teenage discos and later to the local nightclubs, which was nice.

We lived in Glenisland until I was about three years old, and then we moved into Castlebar. I went to the local national school and then to the convent just up the road. I used to go to the teenage discos with my sister in the local hall when I was about fourteen or fifteen, but I don't remember feeling any different to any of my friends. I didn't start going out with anybody seriously until I was about eighteen as none of us had more serious relationships when we were younger. There would have been a group of about five or six of us, and if boys came over to talk to us, they would talk to us all as a group. I can't say that I had any negative experiences. Maybe it was because I was the only one that was kind of different; I'm not sure. Also, we were born and raised and had always been in Castlebar, almost part of the furniture really, so we weren't outsiders in any sense.

I have three sisters and one brother. Many people mix up myself and my sisters. When I won the Rose of Tralee last year, people used to approach my younger sister and congratulate her. In the end, she used to just say, "Thanks very much." It was easier than to keep explaining to them. I don't think that we look that much alike. I see the physical differences between us that other people, strangers maybe, would not notice, because we all have the dark skin, very dark hair and dark eyes, and we are all pretty much the same height. Even though I'm five foot nine, I'm actually the smallest of the family. My brother is six foot five. My mum was five foot seven, which was exceptionally tall for a Filipina. My aunts and uncles on my mother's side are all five foot two or five foot. My dad is five feet eleven — so between the two of them, all of us children are fairly tall. People that don't know me are inclined to automatically think that I must look like my mum because of being dark, but people who know my father's family would see resemblances and traits from his side of the family. I am supposed to resemble my late grandfather on my father's side.

Today the population of Castlebar is about 10,000, but when we were growing up there, it was a much smaller place. I don't remember people of other ethnic backgrounds around the town. When I was in secondary school, everyone was white. I would have been the darkest in my class. There was just one other lady from the Philippines married to an Irishman in the town, and they have no family. She happens to be my sister's godmother and has lived there for as long as we have. Since then, just one other Filipino family has come to live there, and they are also friends of the family. There are about 500 families from the Philippines in the whole of Ireland, and most of them live in the Dublin area. We meet up with them once a year at a big reunion that happens around Christmas time and is a chance for everyone to get together. Even now, there are only a few people of other ethnic backgrounds in Castlebar. I sometimes see an African family in the local supermarket, but that is about it really. I don't know why, but I suppose the majority of people tend to live around Dublin and don't seem to go down to the west.

So in school I was the darkest, and I wasn't even that dark. From time to time, people ask me if I felt different and, no, I didn't. I was never treated badly or differently, and I have no memory of feeling different. I always had loads of friends in school. I don't think any of my brothers or sisters were made to feel different either. I never remember them coming in from school crying because of something that was said to them or because somebody was nasty to them. There never was any problem like that. In fact I only have good memories from childhood. Other children would say, "Oh, you've a lovely tan. How did you get it?" I would tell them about my mum. And then they'd want to know about my mum meeting my dad, and it was such a nice story and one that people always wanted to hear. So I didn't have any negative experiences at all really.

Now, if I'm in a situation where I get a taxi, the driver might be staring slightly because I suppose I'm more exotic looking than the average. We'd start talking, and all of a sudden — well, I have a very Irish accent — he will probably be curious because maybe he expects me to speak differently, and you can see him wondering, *Where is she from?* I'll tell him I'm from Mayo, and he'll invariably say something like "Oh, bet you don't see many people like you in Mayo."

Sometimes if I'm somewhere, like in parts of Dublin, I see African people walking along; then you get these young boys shouting at them to go back to where they came from. It's terrible. That is the very negative side of it. These poor people, and they just seem to put up with it because they just keep walking without saying anything. I suppose there isn't much they can do about it. At times like that, I feel it must be so difficult to try and build a life in places like that with people who have that kind of upbringing and attitude. It is so hard for them.

College and beyond

I left home at nineteen to study, but I hope to go back down there to settle eventually. I'm not so keen on Dublin but I love Trinity. I always wanted to go to Trinity and was delighted to get the chance. I think it's a special place because the atmosphere is so good, and then I've made very good friends there as well. The class numbers are small so everyone gets to know everyone else, and the grounds and the buildings are beautiful. I just like doing things like sitting out on the lawn and reading a book. I started a master's degree course in molecular medicine, which is a year-long course. Just now, I have no plans for the future, just for the immediate twelve months. My degree was in biochemistry; so after this master's degree, I would be qualified to work in a hospital laboratory or in the pharmaceutical industry or something like that. I've always liked science, and I feel that I might well end up working in that area. I like lab work. I'm quite happy to be left in the lab from nine to five. I quite like working on my own, and apart from that, it can be very exciting to get results. There are more opportunities in the field of science all around the country now.

I commute from Maynooth every morning. Maynooth itself is a nice little village, a university town really. It's small, but you have all the basic things there. It's attractive and we like it there. It is my sixth year being in Dublin. I like it, but I don't think that I would build my house here. I like the west of Ireland better, and I can see myself building a home in Castlebar. Dublin is nice when you are single, but I don't think I would live here permanently. Maynooth is a lovely place, being near enough to Dublin yet far enough away to believe that it is in the country. And, of course, it is on the road to Castlebar.

A death in the family

My mother came from a small island called Antique in the province of Visayas. That's where she was born and raised. The island would be quite rural, and people made a living from farming and fishing. They grew their own crops and were largely self-sufficient.

My mother came to Ireland with the intention of spending just one year. She was in her early twenties and came to work for a year as an au pair as many young women do. She was living with a family in Dublin who had a holiday home in Ballycroy. The family and my dad's family were mutual friends, so the two of them met, fell in love and married. Then I came along, so she never went back. She was the only one in her family to leave the Philippines.

My mother had two sisters and two brothers. Their families are all at the secondary school or university stage now. None of them has visited Ireland yet. When they finish their studies, I'd like them to come and see what it is like on our side of the world.

My mother died in March of 1987. I was ten at the time and the youngest girl was three years old. I was in fifth class when she died. It's always tough to lose a mother, but especially so when you are a child and you don't have any understanding of what has happened. My mother suffered an aortic aneurysm. She didn't smoke, she didn't drink and she had no health problems and no warning. She got a pain at 11am on a Friday morning, Friday the 13th. The little girl wasn't at school, so Mum sent her to a neighbour and asked the neighbour to phone the doctor. By the time she was brought to the hospital, she was dead. I think today, if they detected it in time, it would be treatable, but twelve years ago they didn't know as much about the condition. She was gone before they even knew. It was very sudden, but that's life I suppose.

It was difficult for my father also. He was in Bord na Mona, working different shifts every week. But we managed. We were very lucky in that Dad kept us all together. I imagine it would have been easier at the time if we were all separated, but Dad was adamant that we would stay as a family unit. He was very good in that way. I couldn't imagine not having my sisters and brother around. It's a tragedy when a parent dies, but it's also tragic when siblings are separated from one another.

My father was used to being out at work, being the breadwinner, and all of a sudden there were five young children that he had complete care of. We did have a housekeeper for a couple of years, until I was about fourteen or fifteen, then we took over the running of the house ourselves. I cooked, somebody else dusted and somebody else hoovered, so we all chipped in. My father became everything to us, mum as well as dad. Prior to my mum dying, I don't think my father ever cooked, but now he does a lot of cooking, and he has got better and better. Before, I don't think he could fry an egg properly. It's funny what you can do when circumstances change. You become good at all sorts of things that you would never have dreamt you could do.

My paternal grandmother lives in Ballycroy, where my father grew up, so after my mum died she used to come up to visit. He has a sister and brother in Ballina and another brother in Galway. Initially, they were around quite a bit, but after a while we didn't see them that much. It was really my father who looked after us. The rest of the family had their own lives and their own responsibilities. We were lucky to have a very good father.

I suppose, being the eldest, I had more responsibilities, particularly with my mother dying. In some ways I took on the mothering role when my mother passed away. But then I've always regarded myself as fairly sensible and level-headed. But growing up and being the eldest child, there were also more restrictions. I notice now my sister who is seventeen and the youngest seems to have more freedom from my dad than I had when I was their ages.

The Philippines

The year after my mum died, 1988, my father took us out to the Philippines for a month. We visited Antique and met our grandmother and aunts and uncles. Before that, when my mother talked to us about the Philippines, it seemed like a million miles away, which it was in a way. To us it was going to the far side of the world, with an eighteen hour flight and all of that.

Dad felt he had to do it at that stage because we had just got over the loss of our mother and we didn't really know anything about her side of the family. A lot of people told him at the time that he was crazy. I mean, to bring five small children halfway round the world, the youngest of whom was just four years old at the time, was a big undertaking, financially as well as every other way. I'm glad that he didn't listen to the people who told him he was foolish to even think of doing it, as it established that bond for us with aunts and uncles and cousins. I think it was very important for all of us to go at that time. As far as my mum's family were concerned, she had gone to the ends of the earth, and so it was important for them to meet my father and to see all of us.

After I won the Rose of Tralee, the seven of us [including her boyfriend Patrick] went back to the Philippines after an interval of ten years. To us older ones, it didn't seem like ten years. The memories of the first trip were still alive, and we had kept in touch all the time with letters and phone calls, and in many ways it felt like only a short passage of time rather than several years. We met my grandmother, although, unfortunately, she passed away in September 1999. My grandfather had died within a few days of my mother dying. They were writing to tell us that he had died at more or less the same time that we were writing to let them know about her death.

Patrick liked it so much that he'd like to live there. For myself, I'm not so sure. It's such a different culture and, as far as I'm concerned, Ireland is home. I would like to go and live in the Philippines for maybe a year or so and to learn the language. We loved it, but I couldn't see myself settling there permanently.

My grandmother had lost her sight about two years before and had gone to live with my aunt. My aunt lives about seventy kilometres north of Manila, so there is nobody left on the original home place on the island where my mother was born and grew up. The place where my aunt lives, San Fernando, is a town the size of Castlebar with a population of about 10,000 people. They live about a mile outside of the town, so it is quite rural. A lot of people commute in and out every day to Manila, which is only an hour's drive away, to work or college or whatever.

On the second trip we stayed for five weeks and we did a lot of touristic things. We toured a lot in the Northern Province and went for trips to the coast. In December and January it's not rainy or too humid and the temperatures are lower than in May and June, but it still was very hot to us.

The lifestyle of most people is quite western in many ways. Many of my cousins go to college, and their lifestyle is very like the lifestyle of an Irish student in terms of the life they lead and the clothes they wear and so on. People still cook Filipino food, but if you fancy Dunkin' Donuts you can just go down the road and pick up some of that, too. Seventy-five per cent of the population is Catholic, and the rest are a mix of different religions. People seem to take Catholicism more seriously in the Philippines. The two occasions when we visited there coincided with Christmas and the New Year, and their religious celebrations seemed somehow more devout. Here Christmas seems to be that bit more commercialised and materialistic at times. In the Philippines, people seem to spend more time in church, and religion seems to be quite important to them.

The Rose of Tralee

Both my paternal grandparents are from County Kerry, and a lot of family still live in Killarney and in Tralee. I never really knew either of my grandfathers. My Irish grandfather died in June 1980 when I was four, and even though I have photographs taken with him, I don't remember him that well. So my Irish granny is the grandparent I know best. My grandfather, her husband, was a school-teacher who was transferred to Mayo where he got the job of principal in the school in Ballycroy. But even after sixty years of living in Mayo, and although my grandmother loves Mayo, she is still a Kerrywoman at heart. If there is a Kerry match on, she puts up all her flags and decorates all the windows. My granny was one of the first people on stage when I won. I don't know how she managed to battle her way through all those people, but she did. The crown just kept falling off, and she was one of several people helping to put it back on that night.

We all used to watch the Rose of Tralee on the television, and sometimes in the summer we went down to Kerry for a holiday and to visit the family in Tralee, so we were often there at festival time. I can always remember as a small girl watching a float parade on a Sunday afternoon and standing there waving to the Roses. So watching it afterward on television, after having actually been there, seemed wonderful to us.

A few years later, both my father and my grandmother were always saying I should enter. Some time passed and I thought to myself, *I'll give it a go.* I entered the Mayo Rose, but I never really imagined that it would go any further. Then I won the Mayo Rose and it just went on from there. After that it was a case of getting ready for the Galway regional final, and then it was preparing to go down to Tralee and the whole event down there. It was great fun and very exciting. It was great to meet all the former Roses. It was nice as well to see all the variety and so many people coming from all over the world yet with this common bond between us all. People keep coming back year after year, so you have a large group of people who are all connected. There were former Roses and mothers of Roses and brothers of Roses and so on. I'll go back next year and the year after if I'm around.

The year I entered was the first year that Marty Whelan was acting as master of ceremonies. He was very kind and supportive of all the Roses prior to the big night. My dad and other family members and my granny and aunts and uncles were all there. I had a lot of support from Castlebar and from Kerry and, of course, from Galway, as well as other places. It's important to have that support and to know that somebody is going to cheer for you no matter what happens.

When you look at the Rose festival on television, you just get to see each girl for five or ten minutes at most. And, yes, we all look very glamorous in our ball gowns and our make-up, but they spend a lot of time with us behind the scenes, talking to us individually and in group interviews, and we attend different functions. I suppose they are looking at what lies behind the glamorous faces and all of that. So what you see on television is just a snippet of a much longer process, and it is not based solely on appearances.

In my year, there were thirty-three Roses; only seven were from Ireland and the rest from all around the world — from places like South Africa and Dubai and Australia. They would talk about their home places and the jobs they do, and it was lovely listening about all those exotic places. I kept in touch with a lot of them. We write regularly and e-mail, and I've been invited to a few weddings all around the world. I haven't been able to go, but the contact is there all the time. Of those thirty-three Roses, about twenty came back the following year from places as far away as Melbourne. Tralee is a whole week's festival, and it caters for all the family. My granny is eighty-eight and my younger sister sixteen, but they could both go there and have a fun time.

When I won, I would have been going into the final year of my degree, and I had to debate long and hard about whether I would take the year off. I decided I would because I thought it was going to be a once in a lifetime experience. I'm glad I made that decision because it meant that I had no ties. I could travel as much as possible, I could go to as many events as possible without worrying about missing lectures, so I could really make good use of the year. I don't know how people cope otherwise. Last time there was one person there who had very good employers who gave her quite a lot of time off, but I could come and go as I pleased.

I decided to take on a charity, which was Trócaire. I know the Roses always do a lot of charity events, but to specifically choose a charity and make it your baby for a year was a first. I felt at the end of the year that this involvement was probably one of the most useful things I did during that year.

Just after I won, Trócaire was launching their campaign "Sudan Needs Change", and they rang the Rose of Tralee office and asked would I be interested in launching it. I knew I was going to pick some charity for the year and stick with it, so I said certainly. I was familiar, of course, with Trócaire. We always had their collection boxes in the house when I was growing up. I also knew that they had done a lot of work in the Philippines. It was a special kind of connection for me, and I enjoyed the work I did with them.

In December of that year, I went to the Philippines on behalf of Trócaire and spent some time in Manila, where I visited projects that the agency worked with. Then I was in Kenya, in Nairobi. These visits were really good because in the course of the year I also visited a lot of schools. The children would have done a fast to raise money, and I would go along and accept the cheque on behalf of Trócaire. They would have collected maybe £100, and it was good to be able to tell them things that I had seen and where the money was going. I think it makes a difference to them to know that the money they have collected is going towards something useful.

Before my year, the festival was run wholly by volunteers. It still is mainly a voluntary effort, but it so happened that in my year a new chief executive officer was appointed and they hired a public relations agency. Some of my work came from the festival office, some from the agency and some people would just ring my house directly. The year was full time. Apart from the work with Trócaire, I did bits and pieces for different charities. Then there were wedding fairs and race meetings and all sorts of things. I worked all week. I remember at the start of the year I was doing three functions every day, just over-working. I had to pace myself, and I found that one function a day was more than enough. If I had been still in college, I don't know what I would have done. It would have been very stressful, and I wouldn't have been able to make the most of it. There was a lot of travel as well. Things like New York on St Patrick's Day. I actually marched in the parade with the Kerry People's Association. Everybody says that the place to be on St Patrick's Day is New York, and they are right; it was wonderful. I was back in America again that summer to attend the Rose functions. It was a great way to see the world and all those places, and then I got to see parts of Ireland that I never knew existed.

Sometimes when I was abroad, I could see people looking at me and probably thinking that I couldn't be Irish because of my skin colour, and later they might ask me what country was I representing. When I said Galway, they always got a bit of a surprise, and they are interested to hear my background.

I'm glad I had the opportunity to be a Rose. Even if I hadn't won the title, it would have been a very worthwhile experience. I came away with a lot of good memories and many new friends. It was tiring as well. Sometimes, at functions, people want to talk to you and take photos, and you'd hardly be able to eat your dinner. You go away hungry and exhausted, and you have to keep a smile on your face. We all have bad days. There were days when I just wanted to stay at home and hide under the blankets, but you have to get up and put on your make-up and go out. It's very hard work and sometimes exhausting. People only see you at all those events around the world, but they don't see you sitting on the train for four hours at a time, trekking around the country. But, having said that, it was a very good year. I wouldn't change anything about it and I would do it all again.

When the year was over, I felt that I had got a lot from it and that I had done my best. You have to go back to reality and let somebody else have a chance to experience all of that. When I won, I was just one of forty Roses who had preceded me, so that was a privilege as well.

Two cultures

My mother talked a lot about where she came from. We ate Filipino food every day, and when we'd come home from school there would be a tape playing, and even though we didn't know the words we knew it was her Filipino music. Looking back, I think it was really important for her to tell us about the Philippines and her life before coming to Ireland. She was trying to teach us the language. Unfortunately she died before that happened, but, of course, it's a very important part of our lives, and although I'm Irish, I'm half Filipina as well.

Growing up here means that I feel that bit more Irish, but I'm very aware of my mother's side of the family. I'm really proud of my ancestry. Would I feel more Filipina had my mum lived? If she had lived, maybe I would be able to speak the language and cook the food. I don't know and I never will. Right now I feel that I am more Irish. It's probably inevitable as I've always lived here. I know somebody else whose dad is Filipino and married to an Irish woman, and she says that she feels more Irish as well.

But when I was in the Philippines, it felt like I was part of the place as well. It was a good feeling, being part of that heritage and culture. When we were there we would have been considered white. Compared to native Filipinos, I am white or very pale. My brother, who is extremely tall, stood out. Little girls used to come up to him and ask if he was a famous basketball player. A lot of the time we were asked where we were from, particularly my dad. People would ask, "Americano?" So we would explain that we came from Ireland.

I didn't like Manila at all. It's huge and very polluted and overcrowded — horrible really — but where my mum was born is really like paradise. There are banana and pineapple trees and sandy beaches and clear blue water. It's like one of those paradise islands that you see on a "Wish You Were Here" type of programme.

I hope, after a while, to have a family. When I have children, I'd take them to the Philippines, and I'd make sure to establish a link between them and the family there. I do feel that it is very important. I wouldn't leave them to grow up feeling solely Irish and missing out on the Filipino side of their heritage.

Overall, I had an ordinary kind of childhood except for losing my mother at an early age. None of my friends had experienced this. And being the eldest, I had extra responsibilities. But the fact of never being an outsider and never having to try and make friends contributed to that feeling of being more or less the same as everyone else. Having lived most of my life in Castlebar, I have no bad memories, just very happy ones. I love Castlebar and I hope to move back there one day and maybe build a house close to where my father is. Although it was very tragic when my mother died, we became very close as a family unit, and those bonds have endured. It really was a very happy childhood with very positive memories.

Andrew

I FEEL I AM BLESSED TO BE MIXED RACE.

Andrew is in his mid-twenties. His South African mother and English father moved to Galway when Andrew was a small child. Andrew moved to go to college in Birmingham a year after sitting his Leaving Certificate. His older brother had already moved to London. Andrew lived in Ladyswell, an inner-city area of Birmingham with a high black population.

The child

We came from Lesotho and moved to Galway when my father got a job there. My mother got a job in the RTC [Regional Technical College] as a part-time biology teacher. Then they wanted somebody full time and they didn't think that she would be able to cope or something, so they got somebody else. From that time she didn't work. Well, she didn't work for a wage, but she works so much. She started giving lectures in schools. People would come to me saying, "Oh, your mother was giving us a chat in school." Things like that. And the whole family, we were known in Galway. There are plenty of mixed-race kids in Galway, but I've never really known them because they all just keep quiet. But my mother, everybody knows her.

In Lesotho, we had lived in the university on campus at Roma, and me and my brother went to school there. I still remember friends from that time. I've seen one guy there in England, and we remembered each other straightaway. The campus school was for all the children of the staff, and there was loads of European kids. When we came to Galway, I went to school down in Salthill. From there I went to St Nicholas', a small Protestant school in town, and after there I went to the Jes. I was oblivious, I suppose, about colour at first, only hearing stories from my big brother, but from around the time I went into first class at primary school, my eyes started to widen a bit more. I started to get a bit more clued up. But I still made friends, and you see, when I was young I had blonde hair. Even now I look more white than anything. When I was a kid, I looked white white. As I grew up, my hair got more and more thick and curly like it is now, so people could see I had black blood in me. From first to second class, it was still all right. Then at third and fourth class, boys got a bit more boisterous and things started to happen. It's just the same as being called "Fatty". They called me "Nigger", but it never went straight there [lays hand on heart]. Well, sometimes it did. I shouldn't lie. It did hurt at times. My brother, he had a lot more problems, probably because he was older when he came to Ireland. My brother was ten when he came, and he had bigger lips and a bigger nose. But you see, for him, when he was growing up he always tried too hard. Me, I wasn't like that at all. I wouldn't put up with it, especially when I got older. If people would say anything, I would chat first and then see what would happen. But from twelve years on, I met up with a group of boys. There were ten of us, and we used to always hang together. Then from about that age until the time I left, it was just me and the boys. They are still all living in Galway. I was the first, actually the only one, to go away.

When we lived in Rahoon in Galway, it was flats for settled travellers, so around the place we had travellers as well. Not only would there be racial comments, but we'd get hassled because we lived there. It's not a very good area, but that is where I grew up, so I didn't mind it. There was this one guy, Curly Bob we used to call him. His father was a black man who used to wear a patch over his eye. I don't know if he was a dealer or not, but we used never see him, nor Curly Bob's mother. Curly Bob must be about my age now. We used to actually fight with him because he used to live in the flats and we used to live in the houses. There was always fights between the two groups. He was all right; I don't mean to be rude, but he was — how could I say — a coconut. He's a pure Irishman. He doesn't see himself as anything else. I see him now, and he still hasn't seen anything else. He hasn't been anywhere except Galway and maybe Dublin. I suppose me and my brother had an advantage because both our parents were very well educated, very intellectual and taught us a lot. We had been to a lot more places and knew our relatives and things like that. And, of course, we would go back to South Africa, we would go to England, so I suppose we were more privileged because we saw a lot more things.

When I was younger, I would be chatting to Curly Bob and I'd say to him, "How come you're so white?" Well, I wouldn't say that straight out, but I would say something like that, and he would say, "Ah, sure I'm all right." He is a heavy metaler and does his things the way he wants and he is happy and all that. I suppose I was thirteen or so when I was asking him these questions, and I suppose, in a way, I was questioning myself. When I would see someone like myself, I'd question them. I wanted a partner or something. But it was a "no go" area with him. I suppose I was always curious.

For me and my brother in Ireland, our environment was different — it was pure white Irish — but, for some reason, we liked it. We absorbed it and learnt from it; but we also really wanted to break free. We wanted to find out more. I think it's up to the child to go and find things out for himself.

My brother was beaten up a few times in Galway when he was younger. He had friends in Galway, but now he doesn't like them any more. I think my friends got to know my mother better. With my friends, I'd tell them, "If you want to come into my house, you respect my mother, just like you respect everyone else's mother." They know that, and when they'd come to the house, they would chat and she would open up to them, and then they would realise that she was just a normal person. They got to know her, and it opened up their minds a lot.

That was one of the reasons why me and the boys never got on too well with others in town. They used to call us the "reggae heads". We had our own band. I would go to London and I would come back with loads of records and clothes, so we were always a bit different. We were strong, all ten of us. Nobody would ever mix in although we knew most people. I suppose we were like any tight group of friends. We could talk about everything. They were open-minded; and they were guys who would talk to me about racial issues and things like that.

In South Africa we have plenty of relatives, cousins and aunts. Relatives all over the place. It has taken my mother so long to fit the family tree together, I don't think she has it finished yet. My father lived in Africa for most of his life. He went there when he was in his late twenties, and he spent longer in Africa than in England or Ireland. If you ask him he would probably see himself — not as an African man — but he'd associate more with Africa. So he wouldn't be offended if he heard me say that I want to go back to my people.

In England, there is my grandmother and my father's sister; and I have cousins who are much older than us, but I don't know them. I don't even know their names, which I'm ashamed of, but then they never associated with us much. It never seemed to bother my father. It's just the way it went. You would like to know all of your relatives, but you are drawn more to the people you get on with.

The cousins on my father's side are all aged about thirty-five or forty, so if we went to visit there wouldn't be anybody to play with. Whereas in South Africa all my cousins are about my age and my brother's age.

My mother has about eight brothers and sisters. Some are half-brothers and sisters. Then she has brothers and sisters that aren't brothers and sisters at all, but cousins, yet they all live together and they are looked on as brothers and sisters. That is why it is hard for my mother to see who is a brother and sister. Then, of course, when she goes back somebody is always going up to her on the street and saying, "Do you remember me?" She might say, "Your uncle had an affair with such a woman, and I'm the result." So there are just so many. I think she is the only one who is trying to keep track of the family. Of course, that is because she left. Then, of course, she is an activist and more interested in family issues and that. But I have plenty of family in South Africa, and I would like to go back because I never have been with my family for too long. We only used to go on holidays there, always for a month or two months. So I would like to go back, even just to learn my own language and to live with my people.

Coming to England

I have lived in the Ladyswell area since I came to Birmingham. I lived in halls of residence for the first year, but that was near to the Ladyswell area. Ladyswell is traditionally a white area for working-class people, but in the past ten years it got very mixed. Ladyswell has the most single white mothers with mixed-race children in the whole of Birmingham, and Ladyswell is quite small. It is not predominantly one thing or the other now. I suppose I'm lucky I ended up there.

It is fairly rough. Almost everyone has a little earner because hardly anyone has a job, and young kids are mugging people like there is no tomorrow. In Ladyswell there are no nice areas. I was looking for a house near to town: I found one near Ladyswell. Only then did I suddenly find out what the area was all about.

For mixed-race kids in England, it's a different story to Ireland. In Ireland, the mixed-race kid will go looking for black people, and when they find them they are often disappointed or treated badly. It's awful, because then they go back to the middle and say, "Now where do I go?" That is why some people say that mixed children shouldn't be about, because they will get confused. I'm sure this happens to some kids because of the situation they grew up with, but I was lucky as I was wide-eyed from the beginning.

Sure enough, when I came to England it was a shock; and sure enough, I'd chat and some people would be shitty to me or whatever. But you have to take a person just as that person. Then you can think, "That person I don't like." I wouldn't say I don't like Ladyswell people because that person is from Ladyswell or I don't like that person because that person is a black person. I'd just say, I don't like that person because he's David and he is a bastard. That is the way I see things.

Coming to England is a different story. It is one journey coming to Ireland and studying, but England is so different. Maybe it is my own fault. Maybe it was from living in Galway because I always hung around with ghetto type people. Street style. I wouldn't seek them out but I'd end up there. It was the kind of neighbourhood I grew up in. And I suppose that was the kind of way my attitude was.

My brother has had a much harder time with work. I have been lucky with jobs. I have never been unemployed, never. If I wake up in the morning and I have nothing to do until midday, I feel ill. I like waking up at seven and know I'm going to work at nine. I'd never want to be unemployed. Not me. I always want to be working.

The first job I could get was glass collecting and washing glasses behind the bar and that kind of thing. My brother got plenty of construction work and often had jobs, but somehow he never kept any of these jobs. Now he is doing a lot better for himself as he went back to college and qualified as a carpenter. He is a freelance carpenter and getting small contracts. He wanted to be his own boss, and it takes a while to get known. I just want to work and get a wage at the end of the week. I found getting work in Birmingham was easy. I came to Birmingham to go to college. I had a choice of either London or Birmingham. I thought if I went to London I would stay with my brother, I would never study and end up doing something stupid. So I thought, "I'll go to Birmingham to deal with things on my own."

Identity and influences

All my friends growing up were Irish. When people hear my accent, straightaway they ask where am I from. When people ask where do I come from, I can't really say anywhere. I just say, "I'm international. I was born in Kenya, lived in South Africa, lived in Ireland, now I'm here." I don't have any Irish blood in me anyway. Sure enough I've lived for most of my life in Ireland, but all the time growing up I never wanted to be a straight Irish boy. I wanted to look ahead. I know that sounds just like wanting to be different, but I always wanted to be strong. There were no other black people living around, hardly anybody: my mother — that was it. So, of course, me and my brother, we thought we must look for something. We must do something ourselves. So we were strong in ourselves and we found out about things ourselves. We knew we were mixed-race boys and we knew where our people were, so, of course, we just did things for ourselves. We used to talk about race and racism all the time, because my mother, she is an activist, so we would always hear it. My father wasn't really welcomed in Galway either, especially as he had a very strong English accent. So we would always talk about things like that. We would watch television. It was always around us. Always there. Of course, I feel Irish in a way because I have plenty of Irish traits. I do things just like the Irish, and I can associate with the Irish just like the next man, but I'd never consider myself Irish. I can't consider myself anything really, because I can't really say I'm South African. I've got a South African mother, but I've got an English father, too. I have only lived in South Africa for a very short time, but that doesn't bother me at all really.

One of the reasons [mixed-race] people move away from Ireland is that the people have experienced the same place until their teen years and then they might want to find out and experience something different: to go to England, maybe, and to see more black people, more Asian people, more mixed-race people; and then, instead of being in the one place seeing the one type of person, to be part of a multicultural society where they are going to fit in a bit more. If you stay in Ireland, you don't see anybody different, especially in Galway; all I know really is Galway. Maybe you have the Indian shop down the way, but they are keeping themselves quiet, so people are going to look for a more multicultural society where it is a lot easier to fit in and be accepted, where you don't have to explain yourself all the time. Just to be in a more multicultural society is a lot easier, a lot more colourful. In a place where there are people from all over the world, all in the one place, you are going to learn more.

Assimilation and separation

In America and Jamaica they have so many different mixtures. I have a friend called Delroy, and he has Jamaican,

American and Japanese blood. He has all of that, but when he is over here he is a black man. He is just as light as me, but here he is black because he grew up in Houndsworth. He would think of himself as mixed race, but his mates are black. It doesn't bother anyone except the black men. You see, in Birmingham there are some people who don't like mixed-race people at all. Some of them are worse than the white racists. I've had trouble with a couple of them. I shouldn't really say that, but Jamaicans are different. Jamaicans don't even get on with Trinidadians; it has nothing to do with mixed race really.

And this thing [of calling yourself black] goes on all the time in Birmingham. If you have any black blood, they will straightaway call themselves black. If that's what makes them happy, fine, but me, I'm mixed race. I'm not black; I'm not white; I'm drop dead in the middle. I feel the reason why some people do that (I've talked to some guys) is because it makes them feel stronger. They want to go for the strong side, the black side. But if you can't see yourself as strong enough the way you are, then I don't know. In America, especially, they are like that. Americans have hang-ups about a lot of simple things you don't need to have hang-ups about. In America, you have the Puerto Ricans, the Mexicans, the blacks, the whites, the Italians — all strong and self-segregated almost. I don't believe in that at all.

Take the adoption of a mixed-race child — it all depends on how willing parents are, be they black or white, to teach the child about the other side. I suppose, back in those days when they weren't aware, the white family would bring the child up as white and the black family would bring the child up as black. Being brought up as black would probably have been much more comfortable for the child, because black people are a lot more accepting of black kids. They take them under their wing.

It is made more difficult for the white family because, I suppose, they wouldn't get support from any of the black associations, or whatever, with the upbringing of the child. Of course, the black family might be bitter as well, thinking, "Why is that child adopted by that family?" But if the child is brought up in a white family and is comfortable, it's OK. When I lived in Ladyswell, there was a whole load of single white mothers having mixed-race kids. Some of the activists are getting real upset about it, these mixed-race kids being brought up by these white mothers. Some of the activists don't like it at all, and the arguments get really heated. Of course, when you come to the age of twelve or thirteen, you stop listening to your parents and start discovering things for yourself. That's what I did, and so did my brother. So whether the child is in a white family or a black family, it's only until the age of twelve, and then the children make their own friends and do their own thing. Basic learning comes when you are a child, but the things that make your character come later when you are discovering things for yourself.

It does depend really on the environment you live in. An adopted mixed-race child can be brought up by a white family, but if they live in the depths of Houndsworth, or somewhere like that, he is all right. He's got everyone around him. But if you grow up in a white family in a completely white area and if you stay in that environment, you will be fine as well, because that is what you relate to. You can see it in some areas in Birmingham where all the kids get on, like in Ladyswell: the black kids play with the mixed-race kids, and they pal with the white and the Asian kids because they all live in the same area. They don't even have to think about it.

I think you should judge people by the way they react to you. I had this Irish friend, and when he came over here he was really naive. He wanted to meet black people and he would love them all, even if they treated him like shit, because he didn't want to be thought of as a racist. He would hear me say, "See that black guy? He's a real bastard."

He'd say, "Don't be a racist."

I would say, "Why, you can see he's a gangster. He's a bastard."

I treat people on how they react to me, or how they are.

And the individual

You can't choose who you love. Love chooses you and that's it. I know this one black guy and he really loves this white girl, but he doesn't want to go out with her. He doesn't want his friends lecturing him, so instead he is going out with this black girl that he doesn't really like at all. I say to him, "Don't let people dictate what you should and shouldn't do. You shouldn't do things because of what other people will think. You should do what you want to do and stand up. And if they don't like it, forget them."

I wouldn't be able to live like that — thinking of what other people think. If somebody doesn't respect me, then that's it. I don't know what it is about me, but I think I like the danger zone. I suppose I like being in risky situations. At the moment I have a Punjabi girlfriend, and that is risky, because if her cousins catch me, they will beat me up very badly. I was beaten up badly one time already. It's all risky. That is just the way it is. I'm not a Sikh and I'm not Punjabi. If I managed to marry her and we had a child, that child would have some crazy background. I don't know if that child would have problems or if the child would be a really gifted, lucky child — so much culture and so much learning. She already had two arranged marriages and managed to get out of them. In some parts of Birmingham, we can't walk together, but that is because of her family and her cousins. There are plenty of Indian girls going out with white and black men, and it is fine for them. I'm just unfortunate because she has a very traditional family. Her family practically own Edgbaston. They run everything. Everybody knows them because they know her cousin, and they know him because he is a tough man. I didn't know this the first time I saw him.

And being mixed race

Some mixed-race kids are troubled and confused through their lives, and they don't want the same for their own children. They get trouble from black people and from white people, so they want their child to be more one thing or another.

There are plenty of people who never open up. There are some mixed-race boys in Birmingham that I've met, some of them practically pure Jamaican, and when they start chatting to me they suddenly open up. They start talking about things they would never dream that they were thinking about. There are a lot of boys who have a Jamaican mother or a Jamaican father or whatever, but when they talk to me they say things like, "I don't like the way that all the redskin boys are so Jamaican. I wish they were a bit more open."

I would say, "From the first time I met you, you were like that."

I suppose they feel that they can say it to me because I am not really straight up anything. Me, I'm different because I love mixed-race people. The minute I see mixed-race people, there is no negativity at all. I see mixed-race people and I think it is great. When people say, "All those single white mothers catching a black man, having a mixed-race kid because it is trendy" and things like that, well I think it is great. I feel I am blessed to be mixed race. I am not just one thing. I have such a lot inside.

Anne

I AM STILL AN OUTSIDER, BUT NOW IT FEELS OK.

Anne lives in a rural part of County Cork with her family. She grew up in London, and her parents divorced when she was still young. She lived with her German mother and had regular contact with her father, who came from Nigeria.

Anne, it appears, had an ambivalent attitude to her father and only came to know him better shortly before he died prematurely of heart disease. The fact of moving to a predominantly white area as a child and being ostracised because of her colour and her relationship with her father left her with a feeling of unease towards black people.

The child

I was brought up in a single-parent family by my mother who was German, but I used to have contact with my father on a monthly basis. My parents divorced when I was very small, so I don't remember him being at home at all. When I visited him, it was usually at his house.

My mother came to England and met my father, who was Nigerian. She got pregnant and they ended up getting married, which is what used to happen in those days, but it didn't work. Later on she admitted to me that she felt very frightened. I didn't understand it, and it was never verbalised, but there was this vague anxiety that made me very uneasy as a child. Often I didn't want to go and see my father, but I always went as it was expected of me.

They both lived in London when I was small, at one stage in the same road. When I think of it, my visits were probably more frequent at that time. Then we moved to

119

Kent, and I would just see him on a monthly basis. My father, quite often, used to take me to visit his friends, but I used to feel very awkward. They would have been Nigerian, and I would really feel out of it. We would maybe be on the underground and he would bump into someone that he knew — he seemed to know loads of people — and when he would meet his Nigerian friends, they would talk in their own language. I wouldn't be able to follow what they were saying, and I didn't like that.

I think that being divorced has a stigma attached to it in Nigeria. He used to get me to write to his sister in a way that they wouldn't realise that he and my mother were separated, so I think his family didn't really know the full story.

My father had quite different ideas about how to behave. He would say, "Just do what people tell you to do" — so as to fit in. He was always very correct, always very smartly dressed, and he didn't like it when I rebelled. In order to fit in, he always complied, whereas I would have been a bit of a rebel. I didn't see why I should do certain things just to please people. He never remarried, which was a shame because he liked children a lot. I think he had quite a lonely life. He died before he could know my children, which was a pity as well, because I think he would have been quite a nice grandfather.

Up until I was ten, we lived in north London, which wouldn't have had such a high black population as south London but was quite mixed. There would have been a lot of Jewish people, Polish people, Turks, black people and Jamaicans. I was very happy in the small school that I went to. In the class, there would have been a boy from the Nigerian Embassy, an Asian girl, a Jewish boy and a Chinese boy, but it was a predominantly a white area. In some ways it was quite wealthy, but again, it was mixed. I think my mother regretted moving to Kent. I'm sure it was quite hard for her as well. We moved because we were living in one room in London and were offered a flat in Kent which would mean more space. After I left home, she moved back to London and is now living in the same area where I was brought up. Times change and the place has changed now. She would probably have been better off staying there.

My German grandmother lived in England as well. She lived with us for two years before she died, and that was great. [But] I think that she would have been quite prejudiced in her own way. She was only not prejudiced about me because I was her granddaughter. As well as that, she thought that my father was a really good man. She used to always say good things about my father. She didn't even know him, so I don't know why she did that, but it was as though we, my father and I, weren't coloured. She was very loving towards me, and I was spoilt terribly. I think that was very good for me. I think that I had quite a good upbringing as far as building up my self-esteem was concerned, but I feel that this was a general thing and wasn't really related to colour.

My mother would never have said anything bad about my father, but now I realise that she was worried about him taking me away. Whether I ever picked that up as a child, I don't know. Even though she had custody, she was afraid that he would take me back to Nigeria. I just remember as a small child, maybe about four, I had a horrible experience with my father. I had been visiting him and I wanted to go home and he wouldn't let me. When my mother came for me and I told her, he lied and said, "She didn't ask." That fixed it in my mind that I couldn't trust him.

Before that it was different. I have photos taken with him when I was very young, and I looked happy. I think he really doted over me, but, for some reason, this incident when I was four made me distrust him completely. I mean, I was probably screaming and crying and he didn't want to take me up to my mother and show that he couldn't handle me, but I just remember that he lied, and that was it. I didn't trust him, and I really exploited him. I used him as a person to get money from, which is sad really, looking back.

My mother suffered from mental illness. I was always scared about him finding out about this and that I would have to go and live with him, so I had to always lead a kind of double life. I mean, I might be staying with other people, but I would never let him know that. I would always pretend that I was with my mum. It was hard to be close to him, and I never felt safe enough with him to let him know what was happening. I don't know if he knew what was going on (he probably did), but you know how, as a child, you are very concerned about being careful and keeping a secret. That was quite hard. I would have thought had he taken her to court claiming that she was an unfit parent, he would be likely to have got custody of me because there was nobody else; so I had to be always very careful.

I remember talking to my father a bit. Sometimes I think we had this closeness. I remember asking him about the weather in Nigeria and about Africa, and he said that he felt the heat terribly oppressive. That surprised me. I remember as a child thinking that all Nigerians could cope with the heat. And I remember him once telling me about bananas. I always liked bananas, and I remember him telling me about all the different kinds of bananas. So, every now and again, he would tell me things, but he didn't say an awful lot. It was like a very closed shop. Sometimes I wonder what it was all about. I never knew why he left Nigeria. At the time, I didn't want to know, and when I did it was too late. I never knew anything about his family. I asked my mother, because she would have known a little more, but, again, it was all very vague.

The visits couldn't have felt so natural. Usually I would meet him at the tube station. When I was smaller, he would meet me off the train, and we would maybe go for a meal. I can remember how I used to be embarrassed by him. He would dress really smartly, like a perfect gentleman. He would do things like open doors and help you on with your coat, but I remember, if we were eating out, he would turn the serviette into his collar. As a teenager, seeing this, I would die. I would always hope that he wouldn't order chicken because he would eat it with his fingers, and I would die of shame. And I know that, according to etiquette, you were allowed to eat with your fingers, but I had never seen anybody do that in a restaurant.

There were some things that I liked about him, and I'm glad that I realised that he was OK. I always remember that last letter I sent to him. They found it on him when he was dead. In the letter, I was arranging to meet him. There was quite a lot of love in the letter because I was excited about seeing him again. So there was a relationship building up.

My father's funeral was a very sad occasion because he lived in just one room, all alone. My mother contacted me to tell me that he had died. I think his body wasn't found for a day or two. It was really quite lonely, just my mother and me at the funeral. And just a council cremation. There were no friends there and no family at all. I went through his address book trying to contact people. There were no contacts for his family, just an address of a friend in Denmark, so I contacted him. No family contact. I just remember as a child writing to his two sisters, but I don't remember getting letters back. I had met his friends, but I never really knew them. I would have thought that he had many friends, but, in the end, there was nobody. Just me and my mother at a council cremation. Very sad.

School

The first school I went to when we lived in north-west London was a small one of just about a hundred children.

I was very happy. Wherever I went in the area, I was happy. Then I moved to Kent, and I was the only black child on this huge estate. Everyone was white and it was horrible. It was working class with quite a lot of prejudice. My mother was divorced, and that alone was a stigma. In my previous school in London, almost every child that went to school was from a single-parent family, but there it was different. And then to be black. They just couldn't understand it at all.

It seemed like everyone was against me. I had just this one friend, this one girl who decided to take me under her wing or something, to stick by me and be my friend. I did have two friends where I lived, but they went to a different school. I had some friends to begin with, but then they all followed the leader and they all turned against me. When I walked into assembly, all of the children used to move away from me. It got so bad and was so obvious that one of the teachers said that I would be excused from assembly, but, of course, that was really side-stepping the issue.

The headmaster there was, I think, so bad and I hated the school so much that I decided that I wanted to leave. I was there for two years and it was very hard. I always made sure that I was top of the class, because if you were top so many times it allowed you to move. So it didn't hold me back. I was very lonely and I would work very hard just to get away from there, so I think I became much more determined because of this isolation. I had been quite bright at my first school, and everyone assumed that I would pass the eleven-plus, but I didn't. It probably had to do with stress and one of the teachers. Looking back, I think he was definitely racist. He really wasn't nice to me at all, and as a child I couldn't understand that, as I had always such a great input from people at my other school. I had always been very popular.

The next school I went to was more middle class. I was still the only black person in the school, but it wasn't as bad. In fact it was lovely compared to the previous one. On my first day there I was so nervous, and I remember this boy said, "You wog," or something like that. And I remember another boy going to him, saying, "Act your age." That boy who insulted me never liked me, but neither did he get anybody else in his gang to turn against me, which was great. It was quite an academic school where everyone was expected to do their best.

The headmaster in the first school wasn't a great role model. He was, in a way, a kind of a slob and didn't appear to have any great interest in the school. In the second school, if they heard of bullying, it wouldn't have been tolerated. It was a much better experience for me there, but I opted out of studying. I always did voluntary work from the age of ten or eleven at a vet's. I wanted to be a vet ever since I could remember. It might have had a lot to do with loneliness at school. But I couldn't be a vet because I didn't go on to study. In a way, I didn't have ambitions. I would only have seen black people doing menial jobs, so I would never have associated a black person with, let's say, being a doctor. I wouldn't have been in contact with anyone like that, so I wasn't aware that there were any more positive role models.

Young adult

I got a job straightaway with the RSPCA. Then when I was about seventeen and a half, I got a job with a vet in north London. I used to commute for the first year from Kent. I worked in a Cypriot area, and all my friends were white. I remember walking along the street with some friends and this black guy called me "Sister". He said I shouldn't be walking along with these white people. I was very defiant. I didn't like being told what to do. I said, "I am not your sister," and I ended up getting into a fight with him, and he didn't like that.

I left home at eighteen, as I moved to another vet's and got a flat near by.

Around about that time, I started getting to know my father. When I was sixteen, I didn't have to see him, and for a while after that I think I mightn't have; I can't remember exactly. At that stage I chose to see him. When I was still working in Kent, he used to have to travel quite a long way to see me, and I think I really was quite important to him. Maybe, in a way, it was a bit too late because as a child I had been horrible to him, but when I was about eighteen I started to trust him and started relating to him as an adult. At times, I used to feel sorry for my father because I began to realise how lonely he was. I realised, too, that he had a bad heart. He would say that he was fine, but I noticed that he had to take tablets. It must have been strange for him that I wanted to be close to him all of a sudden when I always had been very separate. I think that must have been difficult for him.

Anyway, aged twenty-two, I found myself working in south London, and that was a real eye-opener. I had to take the train down. I remember getting off the train the very first time and seeing all these black people everywhere, and I was amazed. It was wonderful because all of a sudden I didn't stick out any more. I had been a little bit nervous about going for a job there because I was thinking, "Maybe they won't want me." I suppose I still carried that feeling with me. Anyway I got the job. I think the vet might have seen my colour as a bit of a bonus because there were all these black working-class customers. He probably quite liked the idea of having a black veterinary nurse for that reason.

There I was surrounded by black people. I remember when I started to go out with my husband, we went to this pub called "The Victoria", and he was the only white person there. He was a bit nervous because he thought there might be a problem, that the black people might not like it, but he was really welcomed there. It was nice for me. I found that area really friendly, and it made me feel good about myself because I didn't stick out, even though from my colour it must have been apparent that I was of mixed parentage. It seems that black people accept you as black even though you are part white, whereas white people don't. White people would consider me as black and would not include me in the white circle, but I never found that black people excluded me because I was part white.

In south London I tended to mix with white people; I was never excluded, and neither was my husband. It didn't feel very English there in ways. Like, you would go out and hear all this reggae music blaring out in the streets. It had quite a nice feeling, and I think it was good for me to work there. There is a divide between north London and south London. People would say that the part of north London where I grew up was quite wealthy. I think it was good to work in a working-class area. I found that the white people who lived in Peckham weren't prejudiced either. It seemed that all working-class people just got on. Everyone was in the same situation, and it seemed to form a bond between people.

Racism

I would have told my mother about my problems at school, but I really don't think that she knew what to do. The only thing that she used to say to me was, "Well, you will always know who your friends are because they will see you as you are and accept you." This was quite a wise thing to say, because the people who decided that I was OK stuck with me and were good friends. At the same time, she used to also say, "Oh, you have a chip on your shoulder." But it was very hard. Kids don't like to tell their parents if they are being bullied at school because they are afraid it will get worse. She probably didn't realise how bad it was. I remember one time I was getting really bad stomach pains. It was all to do with what was going on at school. I think my mother told me to ignore it. That basically was what you had to do.

I think middle-class people can be quite prejudiced; it's just that they are clever at hiding it. They think they are more tolerant, which is worse in a way because it can be patronising. I always find that working-class people will be straight up with you. I have been in Ireland almost five years now, but I had moved out of London before that. In England, I would have seen prejudice in different situations. I have not found that in Ireland, or not in the way I would have experienced it in England. In England, it would be subtle, nothing direct. Here in Ireland, I find people are curious, but there is no malice. Little children might giggle or laugh when they meet me for the first time, but otherwise people just seem to take it in their stride. Of course, I don't know what people are really thinking, but I find them friendly. I think maybe some are quite curious and nosy, wanting to know what I'm doing here and all that, but there is no badness involved as far as I can see.

Feelings for colour

My mother was blonde and blue eyed. I never had a problem with my colour as a small child. I never realised that I was coloured. When we moved to Kent, it seemed I was the one and only black person around, and, in a way, I just wanted to be classed as white. There wasn't any kind of positive image of black identity; it was all very negative. At one stage, I remember thinking that I wanted to be a teacher, and then I thought, *I can't be a teacher because you don't have black teachers.* I think I wanted to be white all through my teenage years — from about ten to seventeen or thereabouts. I think that I would have wished that I were white. I didn't like being coloured because it caused me problems and it didn't seem to have any advantages. It seemed to be really just a very hard thing. I think it was after I got the job with the vet that I started to feel good about myself because they thought I was a really good worker. Once he said to me, "God, you are a really hard worker. You work like a black." And then his embarrassment. And I remember that I didn't mind him saying that.

So from about eighteen I didn't feel awkward about my colour, but, again, it was still difficult. I remember I went to work in Switzerland for a while, working on a farm, and that was hard because the people didn't even know [before I arrived] that I was coloured. I got off the train in the middle of nowhere up some Swiss mountain, and I remember this woman looking at me, just shocked. She didn't know how to react. Also, I found in Germany, when I would be visiting my relatives, people used to always stare. This was out in the country, and I found that I stood out a lot. Originally the family had lived in Berlin, but they moved to a very rural area outside of Bonn. I used to stay there sometimes all on my own. In those circumstances, I would have just preferred to be white; I felt that I didn't fit in.

Tracing the black side

All of the rest of my father's family lived in Nigeria. I did try and contact them. I met this Nigerian that felt she might be able to trace his family. She wrote an article in the newspaper in Nigeria, pretending she was me, saying how I hoped to be back in Nigeria and I hoped to find my relatives — some of which I never said. I must have ended up getting 150 letters or so, all the result of this small article in the paper. The letters came from everywhere. Some were good, genuinely trying to help, but a lot were just wanting money. Some others were trying to embezzle money out of Nigeria. So it was very disappointing. The woman who wrote the article disappeared and left no trace.

Feelings for black people

Even now, when I kind of enjoy my background and can feel OK about it, I am still nervous of black men. This, I think, must have something to do with my childhood. When we first lived in London, my mother had her own circle of friends. She had some Asian friends and was friendly with a Jamaican woman, but, again, I was scared of black people. I didn't like visiting this woman because she always pinched my cheeks, by way of an endearment. I hated that. I didn't have any affinity with black people. From my experience with my father, I think I had quite the reverse, although this feeling has changed. I got to know this Jamaican man. He was really nice and I liked him a lot. He was a really fun sort of person. That was the first good experience I had with a black man. It made me realise that there was a good side.

I still feel that people from the West Indies and from Africa are quite different. I would have had more contact with West Indian people. I really didn't know any African people. Any African people that I knew tended to be more educated. They would have come to study, and also seemed a bit aloof. Maybe the West Indians were friendlier.

Now I try to make contact if I have the opportunity. There is one man living quite near by. I think he is from a French-speaking part of Africa. I always acknowledge him, and I like when it's reciprocated. I notice that often people, particularly women, don't make that connection. They don't like to make that contact with me. I know that I used to be like that, not wanting to acknowledge who you are. It is as though they don't want to acknowledge that they are the same, that they are similar to me. I was like that once, but I feel it is positive to acknowledge your colour.

About a year or so ago, I was at a concert. This black nun from South Africa came up to me. She was asking all about myself. She was so pleased to see me. Now I don't know much about history, and there she was, telling me all about where she was from. She asked, "Can you sing?" I said that I could, but not too well. Then she asked me if I could dance, and I told her that I could but not in front of people. She said, "You must have it in you." It was like a real pride in this African ability to have rhythm. I think I have it but I have suppressed it. But it was so nice. She was very positive about herself. It made me feel really good. And I thought, *I wish I could have that.* To go up to people and make that connection. She acknowledged that we have something in common instead of pretending that there was nothing.

Defining the self

I still don't feel like I fit in, but I don't feel this in a bad way. It doesn't bother me at all when people ask, "Where do you come from?" I never really know how to answer as it is a long story. Sometimes I'd say, "Oh, I was born in London." Some people leave it at that and others wouldn't. I used to say that my mother is German and my father African; now I say my father was Nigerian and my mother German. Then I'll add, "I'm a right mixture; I'm a mongrel." People automatically assume that I come from either the West Indies or Africa. They find it difficult to believe that I have never been to either of these places.

If I had to define myself racially I would put "mixed race". That is how I see myself, and I find that quite a good term. If I had to define it further, I would put African/German. You see, I don't actually think of myself as English, which is maybe strange as I was born and brought up in England, but I don't feel right saying that I am English. Maybe it's because I am in Ireland and the English didn't have a very good history here. I don't think of myself as British either. It is my nationality as I have a British passport, but I don't feel very comfortable with saying it. I didn't feel particularly accepted in Britain, and I don't like patriotism. I think it just causes problems. I think too much is made of it. I mean, I know when I was young I made an issue of it, and I regret not knowing more black people now. I like the idea of things being integrated. I think the more mixed marriages and the more mixed relationships there are the better it is. I would see that as being my position. I feel positive about my colour, and maybe it's unrealistic, but I would like if race didn't really come into it.

Seán Óg

BREAKING INTO HURLING AND BECOMING A CORKONIAN.

Seán Óg Ó hAilpín is a twenty-two-year-old dual medalist Gaelic football and hurling star and recent graduate of finance through Irish from Dublin City University.

The sports commentator Micheál Ó Muircheartaigh likes to use the example of Seán Óg as a progressive symbol for the Gaelic Athletic Association.

Coming to Ireland and first stabs at hurling

It was a totally different world when we came to Cork. It was February, it was cold and it was freezing, and everything seemed smaller and duller. I couldn't believe how dull Ireland was compared to Australia. It was unbelievably dark and completely different to the Sydney suburb where we had lived.

When I started school, I went into fourth class, and I was so far behind. I tell you, the educational system here is centuries ahead of the one in Australia. The biggest difference at school concerned religion class. In Australia, being from all different religious backgrounds, we were separated into different groups, whereas here everyone was the same. The only other difference was that, in the school I went to, everything was taught through Irish.

In Australia, I had never played hurling, although I had played Gaelic football. It was almost accidental that I got involved with the hurling. We settled in the northside of Cork city, up Fairhill way, and I got involved with Na Piarsaigh, the local club. I made friends with a few of the lads and was already playing football. They'd be off to hurling

135

matches, and they'd always ask me to go along, but I'd say, "No, no," because I had never played the game. You know how it is: if you haven't tried something out, you'd be a bit afraid of it. But I was watching them play and thinking, "God, they are very good," and still not wanting to try myself for fear of looking foolish. At that age, the last thing you want is to embarrass yourself, and you are very conscious about what other people think. So I always refused to have a go although I was longing to and I felt that I was missing out. Then one day the coach said, "Seán, why don't you come up the next time we are training." Of course, I said, "Ah, no, Abie, I couldn't," and he said, "There's nothing to lose. If you like it, you like it. Try it out." Now the dad actually prefers hurling to football, even though Fermanagh is a real football county, so he was urging me to try it out as well. So I had a go. The first time I was very bad, but I enjoyed it. Since then I have never looked back. When you start hurling, you either have the right grip or the wrong grip. I had the wrong grip, which is the golfer's grip. Abie and Paddy got me to do the right grip, and I really got involved in hurling.

Hurling is the fastest field game in the world, and you have to be really alert because the ball is tiny. To look at it, you would think it was the most dangerous game, but I feel safer playing hurling than Gaelic football because the hurley is there to protect you. It's fierce skilful. Concentration and so many other skills all come into play. But you have to train for it, because if you haven't played hurling for a week or two, your eye is out of practice, and your first touch has to be immaculate. It's a great game.

All the brothers play football and hurling. The club we play with caters for both games. I went to primary in the North Monastery and then transferred to the all-Irish secondary school there. Starting off, it was just for the fun of playing, but when I got to the North Monastery it became competitive. People say it is all about playing, but really it's all about winning. Going to the North Monastery was a big influence on my hurling career because you get to compete with the best and to play against the best schools like St Kieran's College in Kilkenny. It was a notch above club level. The county scouts get all their players from the school, and they recruit almost exclusively from there.

Origins — Fermanagh and Rotuma

I'll tell you now, the mother is from an island called Rotuma. Rotuma is about 300 miles north of the two main Fiji Islands. When you talk about Fiji, there are hundreds of islands in all, and many of these islands could be quite tiny. The two main islands are Vanau Levu and Viti Levu. Vanau Levu is the northern island and Viti Levu is south of this with the Fijian capital, Suva.

If someone asked me where my mum is from and I said, "Rotuma", they'd say, "Where the heck is that?" so I just say Fiji. I think Rotuma is actually closer to Tonga or Samoa, but it's regarded as part of Fiji. The people on the island have their own language, which is different to the main Fijian Islands.

I have memories of Rotuma where my mother's house was. The sea was just a few yards from the house, a lovely sandy beach and big banana trees. It is unbelievably beautiful. The weather there is tropical, with heavy downpours for about ten minutes; and then the rain stops and the sun is so strong that it dries all the water. Not like here where if it rains at all it's at it all day long. When you look at Rotuma on the map, it's just a little speck. I was born on the island and lived there until I was four years old when we went to live in Sydney. My youngest sister was the only one born in Ireland.

The mother was working in Nandi. Anyone with any ambitions went to the main island to find work. So the mother was working as a hotel receptionist, and Dad was on holidays there with his friends, and that's how they met. Of my mother's family, there are just two in the northern hemisphere — herself and her brother, Peter, who has been in Vancouver for about twenty years now. The rest are all in the southern hemisphere, mainly in Rotuma and one brother in New Zealand. My grandfather passed away in 1977, the same year that I was born, and my grandmother passed away in 1994. Since we left Australia, my mother hasn't been back. She wanted to see her mother for one more time when she was getting older, but she wasn't able to make it. With a young family she found it hard to afford the trip, and as well as that she couldn't just go to Rotuma, because if the relatives in Australia or New Zealand heard, she'd have to do the whole round trip. But it was very hard for her when she got the news of her mother's death. My dad was sad as well, as my grandmother had been very fond of him.

We left Australia in November 1987. We had gone back for a last visit to Rotuma, and then we travelled to Vancouver to visit my uncle, Peter, en route to Ireland. In Canada we were into winter. The lakes were all frozen over. We had never seen anything like it before, except on the television. We arrived in Cork in early 1988.

I thought it was the end of the world to leave Australia. I remember my mum saying to me that we were going to Ireland: to me Ireland was some unreal kind of place, but Australia was very real. It was where all my friends were, and I was already into sport. Every Sunday the dad would bring me to GAA [Gaelic Athletic Association] matches. I remember saying to myself, "Yeah, but it won't happen." It only dawned on me when we were packing and people were coming to wish us good luck that we were actually going. I never cried so much.

In Australia, I had gone to school with Greeks, Italians,

Chinese, Arab kids and loads of Lebanese — a real ethnic mix. I don't think there is any other Australian city as mixed as Sydney. There are a lot of Irish people there as well. They say Sydney is the cultural capital of Australia. Canberra is the centre of administration, but Sydney has the Centrepoint Tower, the Opera House — it's a beautiful city. You can ask anyone who has been there. A couple of friends of mine, people I went to college with, are all off to Australia, and anyone who has been there loves it. I think nowadays young people don't go to the States as much. They get their twelve-months' visa and they head off to Australia.

I think in Australia kids tend to be healthier. A fourteen-year-old Aussie would be much bigger than a fourteen-year-old Irish fella. The Irish are tiny. I'm sure a lot of this is down to diet and weather and the combination of a few things. At home, the mother would be giving out to us about eating rubbish, as she says a piece of fruit is just as quick, and that's what we would be having if we were back in Fiji.

Settling in Cork

I'm not saying that we had no difficulties at all, but you hear more stories of the terrible times that some people have. A few times, as children, we might have been called "black" or something like that, but Dad was cute enough. When we came here, he said, "Look, I have to warn you. Ireland is not like Australia. You get cheeky people, and you might be called names, but you just ignore them." At the time, I remember thinking to myself, *What kind of place is Ireland if this is going to happen to us?* My dad is very respectful of other races. I suppose it comes from working with so many different nationalities on the building sites. If a fella from Zimbabwe or Namibia walked into the house, he would make them feel welcome. He has great respect for other people's cultures and values. Dad is interested in all kinds of people, but you meet some people here, and they are so closed and disinterested.

After being here for a while, I think people accepted me. I think one of the best ways of making friends is by getting involved in sport. In school, because I was involved in sport, they weren't saying, "Oh, Seán Óg, the outcast from Fiji", but "Seán Óg, the team-mate". And where we lived on the north side of Cork, the people were friendly to us as a family. I suppose the fact of Dad being Irish was a big help. So I felt people didn't notice me just because of the colour of my skin but thought more in terms of "Seán Óg, the team-mate". I think that's how we sort of broke into the local community over time. In fairness, I can't really say that we had many problems — it was more ourselves adapting to the weather — but you do hear of people coming to Ireland and getting awful abuse and having fierce problems.

When we came here first, Mum stayed home a lot and Dad was always trying to get her to go out more. Then she was doing things like walking us to school and going to parent-teacher meetings. She is much happier now. She knows so many people and has made great friends. She knows Cork like the back of her hand and has become a real Corkonian. She goes to bingo, her biggest passion, every week, and she mingles in with everyone.

My father's mother is still alive, but his father passed away some time ago. My grandmother is around eighty-eight now and lives up in Fermanagh. Most of Dad's family are in England, and he has a brother in Australia. When it comes to matches, it makes it a little easier for me, because if you had loads of relatives, they would all be looking for tickets, and you only get so many.

The family

I'm the eldest and I have three brothers and two sisters. I have a brother a year younger, Teu, who is twenty-one and a sister, Sarote, who is nineteen. My other two brothers are Setanta, who is sixteen, and Aisake fourteen, and the youngest is my sister Etaoin who is eleven. Half our names are Irish and the other half Fijian. We are a close family. I am especially close to the brother next to me. If one of us is not in the house, you ask where Teu or Setanta is, and you are always conscious if people are absent, and you are wondering if they are safe. You meet other families who get on well, but the fact that we had to stick together through different things makes us closer than most.

Dad often says that he'd never go back to live in Australia. He had spent time there trying to make as much money as he could to come back here and set up home. My poor mum got the bad side of the bargain, but then she has great guts and character. Not many women would go to a foreign and unfamiliar place.

When Dad was on the building sites, he worked with a lot of people from Cork, and he wanted to settle in a place with a strong tradition in Irish. Funny enough, Dad doesn't have a word of Irish. *Conas atá tú? Slán agus sin é an méid.* Because of living up in the six occupied counties, he didn't have the same opportunity to learn Irish, compared to other parts of the country. For that reason alone, he wanted every one of us to have some Irish. When he was on the buildings, working with people from Yugoslavia or Croatia, they were all speaking their own languages. They thought he was English because of the language he spoke. He used to say, "No, no. I'm from Ireland." Then, of course, they'd ask why he didn't speak Irish. So he felt ashamed, in a way, that he couldn't speak his own language, and he said if he ever had children he would make sure that they were able to speak Irish.

At home we talk Irish or the mother's language. We never speak English at home — it's either Irish or Fijian. My parents' knowledge of spoken Irish is limited to "hello" and "good-bye" and "thanks" and that's it. But the dad can speak the mother's language, so the two of them speak Fijian. We speak Fijian to them, and amongst ourselves we speak Irish. Most of the time it's a mixture in our house.

Cork and beyond

The people on the north side of the city are the salt of the earth. Most people, when they think of the north side of Cork, think first of joyriding and things like that, but you get the kindest people that would give you everything they have. It's important to have two parents who are supportive. I feel I want to give something back for all my parents did for me. They like to feel appreciated, because it's not easy on a mum and dad — Dad bringing me out training and taking me back home, giving me clothes and gear and food and everything. Any success that I have is a reflection of all they have given me.

Dad wanted to move out of the city as he had grown up in the country, so we moved from the north side to Blarney. Blarney itself is a village five miles from Cork where most of the money is generated from tourism. Originally it was a small village, but now it's getting bigger and is very busy in summer. We live about three miles outside the village, and our nearest neighbour is 100 yards from us. It's a good place to bring up children.

I think by nature I'm the type of person who prefers routines and familiar things. I tend not to stray outside my boundaries. I'd love to go back to Australia for a holiday but not to live — unless it was some opportunity in sport. If I got an offer to work in sport anywhere in the world, I'd be gone. Otherwise I'm happy to be back in Cork. I didn't want to move away, but then I did the degree at DCU, so that particular boundary was broken.

You can't make a living from the GAA, so you have to wise up and get a job. When I was doing my Leaving Cert,

I thought business was the thing to get into, as that is where the money is, so I did a degree in finance through Irish at DCU. The person who set up the course is a past pupil of the North Monastery. He came to the school to tell us about the course as it had just been set up the previous year. I was interested because I though it would be great to continue with the Irish.

So I went to Dublin. It was a big change and my first time away from home. The only times I had gone to Dublin was to play in Croke Park, and I was told that it was quite different to Cork. I hated it at first. I was a bit lost as my mother had done everything for me and now I had to do everything for myself. For the first year I lived in digs, and the woman in the house did most things. Then I'd be home most weekends as I'd be playing with the club and county. I love Dublin now, and I got to know the different areas. It's a matter of getting used to a different place. There were just fifteen of us in the class, and we got to know each other inside out and upside down. The course itself was very interesting, but it was tough. We had no textbooks and had to translate from the English text. I think the Irish component of the course gives you that bit of uniqueness, and it gives you a certain identity. At interviews you are asked, "Why did you study through Irish?" I think it implies that students who study through Irish have to work harder, and this benefits the employer.

I enjoyed it. People used to say that I was mad to do my degree through Irish, but I didn't see it like that. I met people from all over — Connemara, Donegal, the Aran Islands. And the Irish was so different. All the dialects are different, but the Connaught dialect is more standard and more pure.

In college I'd often ask people where they were from, and if it happened to be a place with a strong GAA tradition, I'd ask if they knew this person or that person. Often they would say "No," and I'd say, "You have to know him." They'd say, "Sorry, no. I'm just not into it." For me, in the beginning, it was hard to accept that, but one thing I learnt is that there is more to life than the GAA.

I never went out as a teenager. I didn't have the time, but as well as that, when I was sixteen or seventeen, I was fierce shy. At that age you wouldn't be let into most places anyway, so you wouldn't really be going out. When I was about eighteen, I'd go out with the lads, but I was only interested in football. People talk about making sacrifices, but I took it to the extreme: no late nights and complete commitment to the game. It's only around Christmas time, when the pressure of the games is off, that you get out. But I think I used the fact of being tied up with the game as an excuse for not going out. Most of my friends play, although some don't, and it's nice to have a mixture, because the last thing you want when you go out is a post-mortem on the match. I'm not inclined to tell people to get lost. It's not in my nature. I get that from my mother, as my mother's people are very kind, very polite. Because I wasn't in the habit of going out, I used to get a lot of jibes. They'd say to me, "Jeez, you're an awful dry fella altogether." The fact that I had gone to an all-boys' school meant that I was shy in front of girls, unbelievably so. I'd be comfortable with the mother or sister, but if a strange girl came up and spoke to me, I'd get fierce uncomfortable. When I went to college, I really broke out because I was meeting new people, and the only time you really get to know people is when you go out with them.

Declaring for Cork

I have never had a bad experience with the GAA. I think the fact that GAA is now played worldwide — Australia, Argentina, even parts of Asia — has made it more outward looking. When I started, the fact that Da was Irish was a big help. They might have been more reluctant to take somebody starting from scratch, but they gave me a lot of help. I was familiar with Gaelic football, and I probably seemed more involved and more interested than somebody who had been born and bred here. Micheál Ó Muircheartaigh, the GAA commentator, has a favourite saying: "Seán Óg Ó hAilpín — father from County Fermanagh, mother from the Fiji Islands, neither with a hurling background." It shows that Gaelic games are not just for the Irish. I rarely, if ever, had any trouble on the pitch, but I had a lot of praise and encouragement.

At the same time, I think the Irish are as racist as anyone. When someone calls me a name because of my colour, it will hurt me more, whereas you could call an Irish person anything. This could happen on the pitch or elsewhere, but not often. When I hear some stories, I say to myself, *Thank God that doesn't happen to me.* Maybe people say things and I don't hear them, but I've got to the stage where I say to myself, *To hell with it. Why get worried about that kind of thing?* If it happens to me on the pitch, it just makes me twice the person that I am, because it's so stupid. It hasn't happened to me in ages. I think under-age level, where you have lads of twelve and thirteen, it's more likely to happen.

In the summer I go really dark. The first few summers when I came to Ireland, I felt I really stood out from the other kids. As a child, people used to say, "You're not from here," and I'd say "No." They'd ask where I came from, and I'd say Australia. If it was at school, they would then take out the map of Europe, saying, "You're from Austria?" I'd have to say, "No, I'm not from Austria. Much further away."

After winning the All-Ireland last year, people used to pick us out as playing for Cork. I tend to stand out from the others because of my colour, and people might say,

"He's not Irish anyway." When people ask, I say Dad's Irish and Mum's from Fiji, and they find that interesting. It happens quite a lot, and if they go to the trouble of asking, you go to the trouble of giving them an answer. If you start avoiding, it makes things worse. I try to be polite, and I suppose if I was in their shoes I'd be just as curious.

Usually when I go out now people will recognise me from playing with Cork. It's both an advantage and a disadvantage to be known. You do get a lot of attention. When I go into town, people will always stop me and say, "I saw that match. You're from Fiji, aren't you?" I'm used to it by now, and most people are delighted by the success of the teams, so it's gratifying when Cork win. People say to me, "You may as well enjoy yourself now, because when your playing days are over, you are soon forgotten about." The way the game is going now, by the time you reach thirty, you are viewed as an old man. I have seven or eight years to go, and when I am finishing up there will be other players coming up.

If I could make a living from sport, I'd certainly do it. Australia is great in that way as there are plenty more opportunities to make sport your career. If I was offered a book on the one hand and a football on the other, I'd always go for the football, every time. I suppose we all have different talents, but my first love is sport. I know there is a lot of talk of the GAA going professional, but I don't see it happening because its structure wouldn't suit professionalism. I know the GAA make a lot of money, but I don't think that it has the financial resources to pay the players. As well as that, you are loyal to the county jersey, and there is great pride in the parish or local area or the county. If the game was professional, you could be transferred to, let us say, Tipperary, and where is your allegiance to Cork then? With soccer, your attachment is to the club you play for and the transfer system operates. I don't think it would work for the

GAA. Tipperary is the rival county, and can you imagine getting transferred to Tipperary? It just doesn't work. You represent the people of Cork and the people of Cork alone when you are wearing a Cork jersey.

The GAA is really a twelve-months' commitment with the county or the club. The All-Ireland finals are in September, and a week later most players are back playing with their clubs. There is supposed to be a break in November or December, but that is only for the county scene. I love it, and I wouldn't swap it for anything else in the world, I enjoy it so much. I meet great people and make great friends, and that, for me, makes it more special than the medals that you win. If there wasn't a match on a Sunday, I don't know what I'd do. It gives you something to look forward to every week, and it shortens the week just thinking about it. People involved in sport seem to me to be a special breed of people because it demands dedication. People who are not involved in sport have no appreciation of the commitment involved. I have the greatest respect for other sports people. It's amazing the sacrifices that people make for sport. I see married people and they barely see their wives and families. They leave home at 8am for work and go straight to training after work. But sport is a training for life and it makes you mature as well. Training is hard. In winter it's dark at 4pm, and you have to go out into the dark, wet night and just do it; but it keeps you going as well. I'm involved in a team sport, but I don't know how individual sports people get by. I've great admiration for solo-sports people like boxers and athletes. It's just them and a huge pitch. Can you imagine the motivation they need?

We live in a society that is sometimes not very attractive to young people today. I think sport is a good antidote for drugs and alcohol because it demands a commitment. I think that, maybe because of the climate, generally in

Ireland people tend to lead less healthy lifestyles than, let's say, in Australia. Even if I wasn't involved in sport, I'd still be doing something to keep myself fit, because if you are fit, you are confident and you feel good.

I think the fact that I never got anything easy in life has made me, in a way, what I am. When I say I had a hard childhood, I don't mean that my mum or dad mistreated me, but I had to go through a lot of changes. If you think about it, born in Fiji, leave Fiji and go to Australia. Then leave a place that you thought of as paradise and come to Ireland to an all-Irish school with no word of Irish. Looking back, everything was a battle, even though it didn't seem like that at the time. It only seems tough when you talk to other people and realise that they didn't go through all those dramatic changes. But it's the only childhood I know. Things being tough means that I appreciate what I've achieved. Even with college, it's a mystery to me how I got an honours degree. I had to work hard for it. With everything I did, I had to work hard to the extent that it gave me a kind of work ethic.

As I said, my dad had warned me way back, saying, "Look, you'll get a bit of hassle. Some people are ignorant. Just be prepared for it." So I was prepared for it. It hasn't been a problem, and it doesn't really happen now with being in the public eye. People appreciate what I've done. We have given them something to cheer about on the football pitch, which they didn't have for a long time, and the fact that I've contributed to that success rubs off on me. At the moment, I've taken a bit of time off before starting my first job, and I've been asked to do things like opening shops and presenting medals because of winning the All-Ireland. I'm happy to do it because I was small once. I remember when I was twelve years old and Cork won the All-Ireland and I went out to look for the players' autographs. Today's small ones are the future of the GAA, and people generally appreciate the fact that you make time for them. It's nice for my parents, too. When my mother is at a match, people go up to her and say, "You must be Seán Óg's mother. You must be proud of him." And that's nice. But I hear other stories and I'm thinking, *That really can't happen, can it?* Maybe it's different elsewhere.

My childhood made me conscious of people's differences as well. When we came to Cork, we were very aware that you have to be polite to people because, if you are not, they will be thinking, *Who does that fella think he is, coming in here as an outsider?* The feeling of being an outsider has changed this year. When we won the All-Ireland, I declared myself a Corkonian, fully-fledged, with an All-Ireland medal. Now I'm part of that group of people who won All-Ireland medals for Cork.

I see myself as more Irish, to a degree, but at the same time I wouldn't neglect my mother's influence and her roots, because some of them are in me. Dad has a short fuse. I take more from my mother's side. I'm more gentle and kind, like my mother. The values I get from her are important to me, because they make me who I am, but I see myself as Irish. I think when you go to a new place, you go through the mill, you work hard and after a while you break in and people accept you for who you are. I'm happy that people accept me for where my parents come from and for who I am.

Lorna

IF YOU ARE MIXED RACE, WHETHER IT IS A QUARTER OF YOU OR WHATEVER — YOU ARE BLACK.

Now in her mid-thirties, Lorna was adopted by a family with two boys and a girl. Even as a child, she had a deep antipathy towards being stared at or being pointed out as being different. She left Ireland in her early teens, and her only contact with the country is her deep bond which she maintains with her adoptive mother.

In her early years, Lorna fell in love with America and dreamed about the long straight highways and the vastness of that country. A year after this interview, which took place in London, Lorna moved to live in Miami as she had planned.

Childhood and feeling different

I always knew I was different. I was born in Holles Street Hospital and was taken from there to a mother and baby home on the Navan Road. I always knew that feeling of being different, as far back as I can remember. I know my [adoptive] mum told me fairly early on that I was adopted.

I know that Ireland has changed now for other black people growing up there, but I felt very isolated. People staring all the time was what I couldn't take. I had been conceived in London, and I often wondered why my [natural] mother couldn't have just stayed on and allowed me to be born there. I think it would have been a lot easier, although I can't really generalise about that because it does depend on the child. I know that some people have no problem with it, but I happened to be one of those who did. As well as that, there was the fact of not knowing

151

where I came from. Actually, I didn't even know that my [natural] mother was white until I was about thirteen. Up to then, I always thought she was black, and then Mum told me, "No, she's white." I had always known that my father was black, but I never thought that I would be able to find him. From that time, I felt I had a chance of finding my mother and maybe her family; but when I went to look for her, I found out that she was dead.

At school I did have friends. I was the one who would stand up and speak my mind to the teacher. I knew what I wanted and nothing was going to stop me, but the constant staring always upset me. It's not even racism. I'd say it is more ignorance, so I don't blame them, but it doesn't make it any easier either when you are going through it at the time, and especially when you are young. That was what made me want to get away from Ireland. People used to admire things about me, but I could never see what they saw. I used to run, and people would say I was a very talented athlete; and when I was small, I went to dance classes and ballet classes. I won loads of prizes, but they didn't mean anything to me. I just ran and I just happened to come first, and to me that was nothing special.

Childhood and family

Mum is the kind of person that just loves kids, all kinds of kids. I think she just wanted to give a child a home and that was the reason why she wanted to adopt a child. It happened to be me and it happened that I was a different colour and she went for me.

Gloria was five years old when Mum adopted me. There was my brother and then a younger brother and me. My brothers and I get on OK. With the younger one, there is a bit of an age gap. When I was sixteen and left home, he was eleven and had a high-pitched voice; and when I went back to Ireland the next time, he was twenty-five. Even as a kid, Gloria didn't like me, but I though we got on all right as kids. I just thought of her as my big sister, but looking back now, I think she always had an underlying resentment towards me. Now and again, she would just explode and say to Mum, "You love her and you never loved me," and that kind of stuff. Which just wasn't true.

Looking back, it probably wasn't easy for her when I came along as a baby, but we are adults now, and I think you should just let the past be past and just accept it. She got on with her father. He hated me. I got on better with Mum. To me this made the balance even. Gloria doesn't see it like that at all, but that is how I see it. He loved her and did everything for her and did nothing for me. She is very like her father in that he could never admit to being wrong in any way.

Me and him didn't get on. I don't think he had any prejudice in the beginning. It was just that a bond developed between me and Mum which he resented. Gloria resented that as well, but he took it out on me. Maybe as a young child things weren't so bad, but as far as I remember we always used to fight. I ended up hating him. I hadn't spoken to him since I was twelve years old. Even if I phoned Mum and he answered the phone, I'd say, "Can I speak to Mrs McCourt?" and if she wasn't in, I'd hang up.

Even when I went back that last Christmas, he could have said something. I know I could have said something to him as well. He had cancer at that stage and he knew he was dying. He could have said something directly to me about what happened all those years ago, but he never did. He would say to Mum, "Does Lorna want to sit here?" but he wouldn't say it to me. That frustrated me even more. Part of me wanted to have it out with him once and for all, but I couldn't find the words, and obviously now it's too late. Even though I knew he was dying, I couldn't speak to him, but, at the same time, I wasn't rude or impolite —

for Mum's sake. On Christmas day there was a bracelet under the tree. I thought Mum got it for me, and she said, "No, we got it together." Then she said, "Go in and thank him." And I did. And that was it. He didn't say anything to me. I suppose he wanted to but he couldn't, and I do understand that, but it doesn't make it easier. He could have said something about why he treated me so badly all those years. Not saying I would have forgiven him, but maybe I could have understood, and maybe he might even have gone to his grave with some peace of mind. Apparently he wanted Gloria and me to get on, but there really isn't much chance of that.

Mental and physical abuse — that is how he treated me. Many times I wanted to kill him, but I liked my life too much. Besides that, I wanted to go to America and get out of Ireland, and I knew if I did something wrong I'd be stuck there for ever. I felt he just picked on me all the time, and yet I'm the one who gave less trouble. I'm not saying I'm an angel, but I never brought the police to the door or caused my mum that kind of distress. I was the one who always tried to help with the dishes or helped Mum around the house, yet I got the blame for everything, and I found that very unfair.

Mum was always accused of taking my side. It was hard for her, but she stuck by me. If it wasn't for her, I don't know how I would have ended up. Mum and I always got on really well, but Mum and Gloria — I don't know. I mean, as far as I could see, Mum always tried to give everybody the same amount of love. I'm not being big-headed, but I'm the only one who seemed to acknowledge Mum's love in any kind of way. In terms of trying to help her or doing things in the house. Ciaran never did anything for her and still doesn't to this day, but it was just the idea that Ruaidhri and Ciaran [adoptive brothers] were boys, and boys didn't do housework. That really frustrated me.

It's not just Irishmen. Some men are good, but generally, as I see it, the women just do everything and the men do nothing in the house. The boys grow up like that, and to me this is so wrong.

I think travelling has taught me things, because I believe now that you don't have to put up with situations. If a man isn't giving you what you want, you get out. Simple as that. I also learnt that love does not conquer all. For me, that is the reality. If you stay in the same place, surrounded by the same people, you'll never know any better. Except for Mum. I'm always in touch with her wherever I am. I know that some people have a big thing about family, but that's not really for me.

London and beyond

I left Dublin and went to London. I booked into a bed and breakfast and didn't even go to my mum's aunt. I was just having a great time. I signed on. First I had income support and then I got some hotel work. Afterwards I travelled around Europe and came back to London, but even by that time I knew that I didn't want to stay in London for the rest of my days either. I have Reynaud's disease and have to live in a warm climate. That's why Florida is so good for me. But from the first minute I was in London, I felt comfortable, and especially when I made friends with West Indian people.

After I was in London for a few years, I went to Nigeria with a girlfriend of mine. Initially we bought our tickets and it was fine, but then the travel company went bust. We were told when we arrived in Nigeria that we could collect our return tickets, but, of course, we couldn't. I had to stay a month after my visa expired, and they nearly put me in prison when I got to the airport. At that stage my friend had gone back, so I was on my own. Nigeria itself was nice but not Lagos. Lagos is crazy. And I didn't feel, "This is my home. These are my roots." On the other hand, when I went to Jamaica I felt more of a connection. The people, the way of life and just all of it felt more me.

I went to a big wedding in Kerrabaha with about 200 guests. Really I couldn't relate to any of it. All the kids would come up and start feeling my hair. I mean, many of the people were really nice and everything, but I wouldn't trust them. I would be very much on my guard. Especially with the guys. My first boyfriend was Nigerian. I liked Nigeria, but I don't think I would go back in a hurry. I was there during the time of an attempted coup in 1985 or 1986. Anything can happen to you out there and nobody would ever know. So I was glad when I got back to London.

When I got back to London, I went to college. It was after I had finished that I decided to go to America. I went in 1990 and went to Miami for the first time. From Miami I went to Jamaica and to a few of the islands. What I used to do was to get a visa, and when my visa was about to expire, I'd go to Jamaica, come back in and get another visa. Then they copped on, and when I came back from the Bahamas the guy cancelled my visa and told me that I had a week to get out of the country. That time I wanted to come back to London anyway. I did come back, but I wanted to return to the States, so I went to Canada and crossed the border and got back in by that route.

Searching

The main reason I wanted to find my mother was so that she could tell me who my father was. When I found out that she was white, I wasn't too interested in finding out about my white side. I wanted to know more about my black side. That was my whole reason for wanting to find her. To me, having to search was a challenge. I never built up too much hope of finding my father even from the beginning, in case I was disappointed, so I'm not even sure if my father is Nigerian. He might have been Ghanaian, but they didn't differentiate back in those days.

Any mother who gives her child up for adoption should give the father's name, because it's not fair on the child twenty or thirty years down the road. I wouldn't be the type to be going around for Sunday dinner or have her come round to me. I just wanted some answers, some information. I know, in the case of some people if they are given up for adoption, then they want to find their mother to ask, "Why did you give me away?" A lot of that is bullshit. Maybe, when you are younger, it's OK, but even when I was younger I never felt like that. If it wasn't for Mum, I don't know what I would have done. I have always had her love, her guidance. She means a great deal to me and always has. Even though we don't live in the same country, we always stay in touch. With some people, when they find their biological parents, then their adoptive parents are afraid that they won't want them any more, but that has never been the case with me and my mum.

So eventually I started looking, but it took a long time. In the beginning, I just got very basic information — just my mother's name and how she had died and that was it. They also told me that she had married and had two children, but they told me nothing else about my family. If they had told me more about her family at that time, well, my grandmother would still have been alive and I could have learnt more. It took such a long time to get that little information.

It was through Siobhán, my half-sister, that I found my uncle, Tom — my mother's brother. I phoned his son and he put me on to his father. Afterwards, his wife said she was glad that I had spoken first to her son as it would have been too much of a shock for Tom. He didn't know about me. It must have brought back memories. Both of Tom's sisters are dead now. He is married to a woman who is part of a close-knit family. He is very nice, Tom, and all his family are very welcoming. They live in England. Tom's son brought me into the house and said, "Well, you are my cousin." Going to meet them, I must have changed my outfit about ten times. I mean, what do you wear? Is it too conservative? Is it too young? I didn't know what to wear. Plus I was half an hour late, which isn't like me at all. I got lost en route, and when I got there the whole family were waiting.

Through Tom I found out about Sarah. Seemingly, my Aunt Jean had a child by a black man called Samuel, whom she later married. Their child, Sarah, was in a home. Sarah is the one that I want to find more than anyone else. I think we had the same kind of life. Her father was also black. I probably know more background information about the family, and, if I were to meet her, I could give her all that information. She was put into a home in Wicklow. I don't know how long she stayed in the home and I don't know where she went to. It is possible she came to London as well. She is twenty-three now.

Family ties?

The information I have about my mother's family is what I got from the agency. A lot of this was actually found through a neighbour who lived beside my mother's family in Dublin. It's a shame really, because all my mother's family are dead now, apart from Tom. My grandfather would only be in his seventies. The whole family is dead, and really they should be alive. That was one of the other reasons why I wanted to find him — to see if there was any kind of medical history that I should know about. Tom has a picture of his two sisters together. Jean is similar to my mother; you would know they are sisters. My mother looked softer, but then the picture was taken around the age of sixteen and she was still going through puberty.

I have a contact for Samuel, the man Jean married, but I don't know if I will find out anything from him even if I do find him. I wrote him a letter, telling him how I got his name and that I knew that he was married to Jean. I even put in the letter that Tom sent them a telegram on their wedding day. Tom didn't know much about Samuel, just that he was in the navy. Even with my mother, Tom doesn't keep in touch with her husband and the children after she died.

I'm in my thirties now, and it has all come together. Being this age makes it that bit easier when seeking out the family. At my stage in life, I'm obviously not a child looking for another family to claim. I have my own life. People, I find, don't feel so threatened when you contact them.

My African side seems a bit remote. I'd like to meet my father and everything, but sometimes I think you can open up something and later regret opening it. I mean, even with Tom, it might have worked out differently if he had been a certain kind of person, but it's OK and I am glad about finding him. Tom could have been the kind of person who would want to see me all the time. He does call and he phones me up, but the contact is something I am comfortable about. It hasn't become a big family thing.

When I went to Tom's house, he had a video made in 1983, and my grandmother was in it. When I saw the video and said to myself, "This is my grandmother," I didn't feel any connection whatsoever. And with Siobhán, I didn't feel, "This is my sister." I think this has a lot to do with colour. I know I would feel completely different if my mother's family were, let's say, black. Then I'd feel fine. She is twenty-eight now, and her brother is a year younger. I have never spoken to him. Actually it was Siobhán who gave me a lot of information about Tom which helped me to find him, and because of that I would like to meet her.

I don't know what she feels towards me, but she does seem very nice.

As for my father, I don't know — if I ever meet him — how I will handle that. I suppose the first thing I'd do is to look to see if I'm like him. Obviously I don't look like my mother. I'm curious — is he tall? Short? What does he do for a living? That was why I was happy when I found out that Jean had a daughter by a black man. There were two of us, and both of us seemed to have the same kind of life. Definitely I'd love to find her. Even if I go back to America, I'll still keep looking for her. The fact of finding out about Sarah and that she is black was a miracle. The social worker is trying to trace her for me. If I find Sarah, I'll be content.

Going back to America

I like America, always have done. All those big roads — something special about the place. Some of the states are lovely, and every state is different. For example, in California I found that people tend to be superficial. I didn't like it at all. The weather was beautiful, but I'd never settle down around there. And the earthquakes! I'd rather be in a hurricane any day. I went through the experience of Hurricane Andrew. You look outside and you see things flying past and the lights going off. I was with a few friends. We knew it was coming from very early on, so we stocked up on things. The sky was black and the waves — God, I've never seen anything like it. The whole force of the hurricane struck at 2am. My car was smashed, but it's amazing, because when I got back to my apartment not a thing was damaged. Some people lost everything.

When I went there for the first time in 1985, I went to New York. In 1990 I went back again. I felt that if I didn't go then I never would, so I went to Miami. I didn't know anybody there, just the fact that it's warm and you wake up to a blue sky every day. It makes you feel so good, so healthy. I feel if I stay on in London that by the time I'm fifty I'll have a heart attack or I'll wither away in a little council flat. I do have some friends there. Last time I went to Miami, it was meant to be permanent, but then Mum's husband had cancer and I knew that he was going to die. I wanted to be there for her.

Now I'm ready to go back to Miami. When I go back this time, I mean to get a permit. The only way to do that is to marry. Back then I was sharing with this guy. We were just friends, but he said, "Look, I'll marry you," but I just don't want to marry under false pretences. When they ask all those personal questions, I just wouldn't be able to answer, but I'm sure I'll find somebody. Then I'll be able to come and go without worrying, and I'll be able to see Mum more easily.

I would love for my boyfriend to come over, but he just can't see himself living in America. I mean, I don't see everything as being good there, but what balances it for me is the weather. That and being able to travel — to the West Indies, to South America, to Central America. My boyfriend always knew that I was going back. I feel that I don't have a choice. I don't know what will happen, but I just know that I will have to move. The last time I went it was really terrible, leaving him. I don't want to go through that all over again, but I know inevitably that it is going to happen. I love him to death, but I can't live in England.

I wouldn't say that, racially, it's easier in America, but it's more open than in England. In Miami you get what are called the rednecks, and they are known to dislike black people, but they will tell you this out straight. Here [in England] they might be nice to your face and then talk about you behind your back. You definitely get that here, and I don't like it. There, you have the American blacks against the Haitians, the Latinos, the whites and so on.

Everyone tends to stick with their own group. You could live in an area that is predominantly black, but you'd get white people just like the area where I am living in here in London. You do have a mix, but usually people just stick with their own kind.

Black/white, self

Where I grew up in Ireland, it wasn't a multicultural society. For some people this is OK and they can deal with being mixed race in a white society, but for me — no. To be constantly stared at and asked, "Where do you come from?" Even if I didn't open my mouth, they would still ask, "Where do you come from?" Constantly. This was made worse by the fact that I wasn't sure of where I came from.

I was watching a programme once about mixed race, and it was saying that you couldn't be both. You either choose the black side or the white side. I agree with that. As you mature, most women of mixed race will be attracted either to white men or black men and will stick with that. I'm not saying that people of mixed race cannot date both, but I am saying that, generally, they go for one or the other. It's something that is in you. I know a lot of white people, but as far as a partner or a lover or a husband is concerned, I would never consider a white man. I wouldn't call myself a racist, but in terms of ever having a child — I'd never have a child with a white man.

It's probably because of my upbringing, because I have been surrounded by white people all of the time. You get a lot of white men who say, "I want to go out with you. I have never been with a black woman." You want to punch the person in the mouth. With a black man I feel more comfortable. I feel that he knows where I am coming from.

If you are mixed race, whether it is a quarter of you or whatever — you are black. I mean, nobody would consider me white. This is why I say there is no in-between state.

162

The white people won't accept me as a white person because I am not white. I get more acceptance from black people. Even if you are mixed race, you are still black. That is how society sees you. Black is black. The funny thing about it is that even white people are not 100 per cent white. But people have different experiences. They might find that they are unacceptable to white people or to black people. I've been lucky, as I've always been accepted by black people, and more so than by white people.

Everyone is different. I don't deny my white side, but I'm not white. To me there is no middle ground. I suppose from the beginning it is society that dictates your position. I think society forces you to make a choice. I'm not saying that you have to deny any part of yourself. You have to be happy with who you are. But if you are black and trying to be white or a white person trying to be black, then that is crazy. You are who you are. If a black person speaks with any kind of intelligence, they are accused of trying to be white. I find that a lot of people tend to think like that and will do anything to put that person down. This is why you have to be strong and get in with people who are on the same level as you.

You know Tom said something like, "People do things and they don't realise what effect their actions will have maybe thirty years later," and that is true. For me, it is amazing opening all those doors, because you can never be sure what you are going to find behind them.

Ian

. . . MY EYES ONLY LOOK OUT.

Ian, a handsome man in his thirties, made history in passing out of the Garda Training College and was fêted in the newspapers as "the first coloured guard in Ireland". As an adopted child, he grew up in a quiet, settled neighbourhood of Dublin where the northern reaches of the Phoenix Park provided a playground for him and his friends.

Ian learnt of the identity of his natural mother at a relatively late age, and this has resulted in a sense of turbulence and confusion about his identity.

Childhood

Your identity is something that evolves very, very slowly, and it's something that you don't really focus on until later in life. My own parentage is Indian–Irish. That's where I come from. I'm in my thirties. In the sixties when I was growing up and in the seventies when I was a teenager, I found that in this country they are more understanding than England because there would be less of a threat to jobs. I think Irish people have a great sympathy towards different races and different people, having been oppressed themselves. They have a certain amount of tolerance, but, there again, bigotry does exist.

Going to school would have been my first experience outside the family. Now I would have been adopted as well. I grew up in Cabra. My mother was a housewife and my father worked in the Ordnance Survey Office all his life, so it was a very ordinary upbringing, and I never noticed anything different. Sometimes you would, but in your own little community you were quite accepted; if you should stray further, people would notice a little more.

I have one brother older than me. He wasn't adopted. We were like brothers, but at the same time I suppose you feel, "I'm different," though I wasn't made to feel different. You just feel it that little bit. You feel a great pressure to succeed because people notice you more. If you do something wrong or something good, people point you out, and you are recognisable wherever you go.

In school there was bullying. Not an awful lot, but I think, over the years, I developed the ability to be able to talk, to be able to respond, the ability to be quick and sharp. I realised that, physically, I wouldn't be able to retaliate. Initially it was a bit frustrating, but then I was able to develop this ability and I was able to laugh it off. It was a self-defense mechanism, and I suppose it just got to be part of my personality, a developed part. Had I not been, let's say coloured or slightly different to other people, I would probably have been a different type of person. It did affect me and it still does to this day.

I was never depressed over it, never angry. Well, I was angry at times, but I never had a consistent regret about it. I was quite happy to be me. It was an advantage in this country where people are all fair-skinned. It's an advantage certainly with women, and it's an advantage to be recognised if you are a decent type of person. It can be an advantage in this job if you are going for promotion or something like that. They would know who you are. It can be a disadvantage as well, of course, but I think overall it's more of an advantage.

I was always a very good athlete. That obviously comes from my father's side, because as they say, "White men can't jump." Ethnic people or coloured people or mixed-race people are better at sport. I was always very good at running and activities like that.

I'm not sure how my parents felt about my colour. My father has been dead for twelve years now, but I never really questioned how they felt about it. I know that they did say to me when I was going to secondary school that they had checked the different schools to see how I would be accepted. I went to Marion College in Balls-bridge as opposed to the local school. It was quite a distance, and I was back and forth every day, but I think they decided it was better. I think they said that they had rung the school, and my brother was already going there, and they had more of a casual approach. There were a few, let's say, mixed-race pupils, but not a lot. I think my parents felt that if I went to the local school I wouldn't develop, as I would be hanging around with the same people all the time and that it was good to mix. I suppose, in the long term, it was better, but I didn't know that at the time. I just went along with the idea that I was the same as everybody else. And you do, because my eyes only look out.

I would, without being big-headed, describe myself as a leader, of sorts. I like to take charge, so I tended to be the leader in my group of friends. When you are good at sports, the other kids look up to you, so the local kids were my friends and still are to this day. They never said anything, and if anybody slagged me or anything, they were quite defensive. My mother would always say, "They are only jealous." Other people used to say, "Sure, you're not coloured at all." I have to laugh at people saying that to me, because I know that I am. And I know that if you put me and someone else together, you would say, "You don't quite look Irish to me." Those people are just trying to be kind, but that actually upsets me more. I'm proud of my heritage like anybody else, and I don't like anybody to take away from it. It's like if you're from the country and someone says to you, "You don't sound like you are from Kerry."

Work and other influences

I've no problem in terms of work. They slag me in work and they always have from the first day I went to Temple-more. A friend of mine who was there before me said that they had heard all about this coloured guard, and they expected something out of the Cosbys to arrive. It was a bit intimidating and a bit daunting, because when I arrived down everybody was out watching and it was like walking the gauntlet. People still watch. Even when you go to court, you find people are watching, and it can be a little bit unsettling sometimes.

Then, of course, I went through Templemore and everything was grand. I didn't have a problem. They didn't treat me much different to everybody else, but I felt that they did use me a bit to their own advantage in some ways. I wondered why they had never employed someone who was Chinese or something like that. It was the first time they had ever decided to take someone on who was from a mixed-race background, in the sense of somebody whose appearance was different. (There are other people that are mixed race but you wouldn't notice.)

They made a lot of publicity out of it. They said to me that the press would be down there when I passed out at Templemore, and they asked me if I minded. I suppose I was kind of naive because I was only twenty-one, but if it happened now I would probably do the same. Later I wondered did I get into the gardaí on my own merits or did they decide at that particular time to open their doors?

There is a [mixed-race] girl who was there at the same time who has the same surname as myself and who joined about the same time. I could never talk to her and she couldn't talk to me, because if we did I felt people would think there may have been something going on. Because we had the same name, people used to ask, "Are you brother and sister?" or "Are you married?" I don't know;

it just didn't feel right. I think she felt the same. I felt that it was expected that we had something in common, and tongues would wag because it's such a close community down there.

Coming out of Templemore, the parents were very pleased and the neighbours and all. They had some claim to fame: this living history walking up the road rather than dead monuments. I was quite glad to go along with the whole thing. I went to Pearse Street, which was a city centre station, and people noticed you. Even years later, people I'd meet on the street would walk up to me and say, "I know you. You used to be on the beat on Grafton Street." I was on "Garda Patrol" for about four years, and even to this day people remember, especially the older people or country people who wouldn't have all the stations.

I think there was a lot of pressure that I didn't realise was there at the time. It accumulated over a period of time. Now, looking back, I think, "Jesus Christ, that's an awful lot of pressure to put on one person." If you do anything wrong . . . You are like an ambassador, to a degree. Another lad might be able to go along the street cursing and might hit somebody a few digs. Now if I did anything wrong and people complained, they'd probably say, "I don't know who he was, but he was a dark fellow," and who the hell is he going to be? So you have to be on your best behaviour all the time. Now that is all right, but it's not fair in other ways. Still, I've got used to it. It has changed me, but not in a bad way, and I think the advantages outweigh the disadvantages. I probably don't use it enough to my advantage. I could use it an awful lot more. Sometimes I become quite angry and bitter. I know there are people on the job who are racist. They don't like anybody who is not Irish, no matter where they are from. I can't understand it. It's sad in one way. There are people who hate anything that is different. They are frightened of it. People when they hear the word "racism" would picture the Klu Klux Klan in America and the American blacks, but it extends much further than that. There are people like that in most countries, for many different reasons. They are people who wouldn't say anything in your hearing, but you'd know it. They would undermine you to other people. Certain people would be jealous when you stand out, when you are different. I think it is jealousy and ignorance. I think people just like to knock other people. They love to see somebody fall. And that again puts you under pressure. They'd love to see you caught for something or in the paper over something. They don't matter to me really, but I know they are there, and it's a bit uncomfortable.

In the job itself, the majority of people are decent people, but they still don't make an awful lot of allowances at the end of the day. Some are still very old-fashioned in ways. They take on something, like they take on different races, but they just take it on and leave it at that. In all the years that I have been in the job, no one has ever asked me, "How are you getting on?" and no one ever came to me and said, "Look, we have had all this publicity: how are you coping? Do you have any problems?" The onus is on me, and I don't think that should be the way. To a certain extent, I'm angry about that. It's not that I got nothing from it, but in another way, I feel that they have used me. And I feel isolated because of it. They could have been more supportive.

I think it was a very important job. I think when somebody says they are a garda, it's like being a doctor and people immediately take notice. If you said you were a plumber, then half an hour later everybody would have forgotten it. You feel part of something. You have status in the community even if you haven't status within the job itself. You may not be the chief superintendent, but you have great power to affect people's lives, for good or for bad. That is very attractive to people, because everybody wants power at some stage.

I think, maybe because of my mixed background, I always wanted to be a garda. My uncle was a superintendent in the gardaí, but I don't think it had much to do with that. I think it had a lot to do with my personality and the fact that I was different. Because I was different, I wanted a job that was different. I wanted something as individual as I was, and I wanted to be in a job that made a difference. Not to be an ambassador, but in a slight way to do something about it, because I couldn't be knocked about any more. I just felt that people who used to slag, well, now I could show them that I was somebody who was worthy of some respect. That might sound like a crutch, but that was the way it was for me, I think. It is exciting and it is risky and it has all those elements in it. I can go out and I know people are looking at me, and maybe people are making smart comments like "Jesus, look at the black guard." But I don't care because I'm the one in uniform, and I'm the one who has the power and not them. If I was nobody or if I was Joe Soap, just working in the builders' providers down the road, they might be more inclined to be more vocal about my colour. In one way it just gives me a bit more safety.

The work is inclined to be bureaucratic, with people being suspicious and maybe always seeing the worst in everything. A lot of that is from the old school, and I think the younger people coming in are changing things. It is a lot less militaristic. People are acting more on their own initiative, and people are more educated. People just can't be merely ordered around any more. Most of the time it is changing for the better.

As a guard, you see what other people wouldn't see. I can walk down the street and I would see things totally different to what you would see. I would notice things, and

I might be thinking, "Yer man over there is up to no good." That goes with the job. You can be a bit suspicious of places and circumstances and what people are up to. You develop a nose for things, and that is a good thing because it is a way of protecting yourself. And you can't turn it off when you go home. You see things all around you, but that is good, too, because you live in a community of people who are different. They like to see the guard living down the street because they say it makes them feel secure.

They slag me in the station I go to, and I take it, but some people go overboard. Some people think it's fun to make racist jokes. And people who wouldn't know you that well, people not doing it intentionally but just not thinking before they speak. You'd laugh at it, but behind it all there is something. When you are in a situation where there are so many different issues, you can't expect people to tiptoe around you all the time. I find the best form of defence is offence. And I find, like when I was first stationed in Blanchardstown, the best thing to do is to slag myself, because I don't want people to be uncomfortable around me or for people to be conscious of this or that. The best thing to do is to sort it out from the start. So I sort it out by going in, and I can slag myself. If you have the ability to laugh at yourself, that's great; but there are some people who can take that up the wrong way, and now and then they can use it to get a dig in. Some people hear things that your friends might say, things that you'd accept from your close friends, but these people would take that as licence to say what they like. Things they say all the time like, "Are you browned off today?" or "Is it true what they say about coloured men?" Of course, I'll reply, "Once you've had black, you'll never change back." There is no point in getting upset over it. There is no point in saying, "Listen here . . ." You can't react like that because you'd find yourself totally isolated. They'd say, "I was only joking," and you'd get a reputation for being cranky. You can get cranky about other things like your work, but when it comes to personal things it's different. People would get the wrong impression if you reacted to it all. So I can slag myself better than anybody else can. Maybe I shouldn't do that, but I like to settle people around me. I like to take control. I don't want people to be uncomfortable around me or not to be able to say things. The unit here is very good. They do slag me, but they get slagged as well. Everyone has something, only sometimes it can be hurtful. But they don't mean it. You have to excuse people sometimes. Nobody is perfect. But after a while you can become quite bitter, because everywhere I go I get the same jokes; they say the same things everywhere. I've heard it all so many times. Sometimes I get totally fed up with the whole thing, but that's only now and again. Mostly it's fine.

Certainly I would be angry with my superiors, not on my own behalf now, but for others. People who would be seen to be different, like people of a different religion. But there are no other officers with any visible difference within the job. There is just myself and MB, both from a different racial background. I've seen nobody else, and this surprises me. Now maybe nobody else has applied for the job, but I find that hard to believe. I know other organisations have tried. I can't understand why they don't have more mixed-race people, because there are a lot more mixed-race people living in this country than, say, twenty years ago. There are a lot more people living here from all over and a lot more black people, and all sorts of people like Italians and so on. So why can't they have representation from all walks of life? I do feel isolated. If there were others in the job, it would take some of the pressure off, but they haven't done that. Maybe they learnt their lesson and said, "No more Ian Brennans on the job," or something like that, but it would be nice if there was more diversity. Not that I would want to band together, but it would be good. At the end of the day, even though I'm not made to feel any different in the job, if anything went wrong, I'd know that they'd make sure that that would be the case. I know I sound very resentful of authority. It's not for the way they have treated me, because I haven't been mistreated. It's just if I was in their position — but then again I'm different to them, so I would think differently. But, for them, as long as there doesn't seem to be a problem, then there is no problem.

People around me who slag me don't realise how dangerous it is for them to do that, because if I was the type who went to the authorities and said, "I can't stand it any more. I've been discriminated against for years. I'm taking an action against you," I'd have every newspaper in the country beating down my door, and they'd make a huge issue of it. Now I'm not that type of person, but they don't realise that there is that racial element to it. It has happened in other forces and other jobs. I think there are certain things I might have gone for but I mightn't have got because of my colour. I sometimes think this, but I prefer to think differently. It's a very thin line, and you can't accuse anybody of being racist when they have discretion as to who gets promoted, but I think that sometimes this is the case. It's not something you meet every day.

I think Irish people are very stand-offish. I think they are frightened of people who are different. Even the way we treat people who are disabled, anyone who is different. In other countries, they are more used to different people. I think Irish people are a bit naive about it. I think, actually, in most cases, when they meet somebody who is slightly different, it is more that they are fascinated and curious. I was away with a friend of mine four years ago in Donegal, and we stayed with friends of his parents in Mountcharles. He went back there recently for the first time since then, and everybody asked about me. They said, "Where is that friend of yours? He was a very nice chap," and they remember you first of all because you stand out. It's a novelty. There isn't any animosity in it. It's more a fascination. And then people say, "And you're a garda as well." That's a real uplift for me that people are interested, and I like it.

Identity and influences

I used to always believe it when my mother told me that the people were jealous and that those people really wanted to be like me and that they'd love to have a suntan all the year round. I don't believe that, but in a way I do believe it still. It was a very reassuring thing to think. So I still use it as a security blanket, even if I don't actually believe it; but it's nice if you have something like that in your head. It can get you through. You know you have to accept that for the rest of your life, as long as you live in this country, people are going to look at you slightly differently. But I think in Ireland it's not out of any malice. Most people, if they see someone who is very dark or someone who is a different nationality, something that they usually only see on the television, they are curious. They'd love to come over and talk to you. They don't have a look of hate on their face that they might have in other countries. I think if people dislike you, they dislike you for something you have done and not for who you are. There are the odd few, but usually by the time you meet them you are likely to be more mature and a bit tougher, and it wouldn't really bother you.

Looking back to when I was, say, between fourteen and seventeen, the time that can bring the biggest changes in your life, I think you are very conscious of being different. If you think, "They are looking at me because I am horrible," that is a problem. They look at you because you are nice, and maybe they are jealous of you because you have something that they don't have, which is an all-year-round suntan. Girls in Ireland love that, but then they might be a bit stand-offish as well because the other fellows would be slagging them. Like a Catch-22 situation. So I think that if people look at it as an advantage, young people especially, it helps to strengthen you. Once you have a close circle of friends that you can bounce things off, then, should things go wrong in other areas of your life, you still have them. I think you need this closeness more than other kids do. I think people who are different need one or two very close friends who really understand them, and if they have that I don't think they will have any problem.

Nothing happened [about tracing my natural parents] for years and years until a time after I had married. Then I though I might try and find some information. I felt, if I ever had children, I wanted to be able to tell them a bit about their heritage. I was thinking things like, if the children of this third generation were very dark, how could I explain this to them? And I wanted to know before my natural parents were too old.

So, about three years ago, I went to the social worker to try and track down my natural mother, just to set the wheels in motion. She came back and said that she couldn't help with the tracing. I was born in London and I was baptised in a church over there before I was brought back here, so I was thinking of looking there, maybe in the church records, as they are better at tracing over there.

Shortly after that, my own mother, my adopted mother, said to me, "I believe you were looking to find out who your mother was?" I hadn't told her I was looking because I didn't want to upset her, so when she said this I was wondering how she knew. I felt it was a bit much for maternal intuition, but the social worker that I contacted had gone back to my mother, and it stopped there. My mother had all that information, and she told me who my natural mother is.

The adoption papers

I was eight months old when I was adopted. I was born in London and was brought back by my natural mother, Mary, to live with a family in Rathmines while my mother was deciding what to do. Afterwards she moved from there to the home on the Navan Road while she made up her mind. My adoptive mother didn't know that her sister, Mary, had this baby, but the eldest sister did, so the two of them went together and told her about me. Of course, she was flabbergasted. It seems the only option was to put me up for adoption, and Mary had left me in the care of the nuns. My adoptive mother's story then is that she went to my father, and he said, "Why don't we adopt?" Reading between the lines, I wonder if my mother had cajoled him into it, as she has a great ability to do that while leaving him think that he had made the decision. My other aunt had offered to take me, but she was already pregnant herself at the time. So it was the three sisters together, and obviously they discussed it amongst themselves. Nobody else knew as far as neighbours and relatives and friends were concerned. I was just an adopted child who arrived on the scene, and that is the way it was done.

As a child, I had fantasies about my real parents. You have inflated ideas. It wasn't that I was running away from something or trying to find something better than I had. I just felt I had a right to know. When I found out and pieced everything together, it became clear to me why my Aunt Mary was always around and why she played such a major part in my life. She was always present for the big events in my life, and my parents always included her. Looking back, it was fine, but it was also slightly selfish in a way when you think of the child's point of view.

I had a very good childhood, and finding out has not made me insecure. I think it has made the people around me insecure. I appreciate what has been done for me by my parents and relations and that they did the best they could for me, as any parents would. They took their responsibility seriously. I'm not questioning that. But, since I found out, had they been a bit more understanding about how I felt, rather than having an attitude of "Well, now you know, let's get on with it. It's no big deal. Plenty of people find out that whom they thought of as their aunt is their mother and there are step-siblings and they all get on." It is very confusing. From childhood you assume that the people who are meant to care about you really do. All through the years, they say, "If you have any problems, you can come to me." And then, when you have a problem and you need their help, it doesn't happen. You think, *What's going on? Why can't I sit down with my mother and ask her these questions? Am I not entitled to know?*

It was in the summer time, when my [adoptive] mother told me that her sister, Mary, was my mother. Shortly after that, I remember my cousin was visiting from Canada. Mary had organised a bit of a garden party. It was my first time to meet her after finding out that she was my natural mother. Of course, my [adoptive] mother had phoned her to let her know that this had happened. At some stage, I went into the kitchen, and Mary was there. She came over to me and said, "I believe you know?" I nodded, and she said, "You will always be my little boy." After a few minutes I left. I mean, I didn't know whether to laugh or whether to cry, so I continued on as if nothing had happened, but everybody else knew that something was happening. After a while, my brother was told. He never knew up to then and he was in shock. My older cousin found out, and he was in shock also. I met him and he was in tears, saying, "All the time we thought of you as adopted, and all that time you were actually my cousin." It was very confusing. My grandparents are really my grandparents. My brother is not my brother, he is my cousin. My aunt is my mother. All those people whom I felt were just people whose family I entered into through adoption were my family all along. That felt good. I thought, *At least now we can all be honest; our lives can open up and we are all part of this family, all blood relatives.* But that never happened.

Mary, my mother said, had been working in the post office before getting pregnant. She told me that Mary had a relationship with a student doctor and I was the product of that relationship. After my adoption, Mary stayed in Dublin for a while, and then she met this man and married him and went to live with him and his children in Tullamore. They had a pub in Tullamore, which they eventually sold and moved to Dublin. Her step-children don't know about me as far as I am aware. I have never been introduced as "Mary's son". It's all cloak-and-dagger stuff. Sometimes she behaves in a maternal way, like you would with a six-year-old child, but this is not the kind of rapport that you would have with an adult.

When my adoptive mother told me these things, she added that if I had any questions I should ask her. That implied that I wasn't free to ask Mary questions. When I met Mary the next time, it was more or less a case of her saying, "Look, nothing is after changing. You are still my little boy and nothing has changed." I thought everything had changed. I remember that meeting very clearly. Here was I, a grown man, but I felt like a child. It's a great leveller, and I certainly didn't feel as grown up as I should have felt.

The missing pieces
Since then, things haven't improved or worsened. They haven't moved anywhere. I've tried on a few occasions to

instigate changes, but they are always blocked. If my natural mother was a total stranger, I'd be able to be less concerned about how she feels. I feel she has had a hard life and I believe I should be able to support her and say, "Hold on, this is my mother. You've had the privilege to be brought up by her and I didn't. To me she is top dollar. She is my mother. I love her whether you do or don't, and I won't see anybody hurt her." I would like to have some sort of recognition of me as a son. I have no inhibitions about it. Is there some reason why she shouldn't be proud? I feel she should be able to let the whole family know about it.

They have an advantage over me in that they know me so well. They know what makes me tick and they know how to manipulate the situation, saying things like "It was the sixties and it was a different time." After a while the record wears thin when you constantly hear them say, "We are all elderly people now." They fall back on the past whenever it suits them. I just want them to be honest. If they feel pressurised, they use the excuse of being old. They never informed me about it when they were younger and fitter. My adoption was legal, but sometimes I wonder who they were doing it for. To this day, my mother defends her sister, and you have to ask who is she doing all this for: for me or her sister? Initially, when I found out, it was a case of "Don't upset Mary", and it seemed to me that she was protecting Mary and not me. Mary is her sister, but she was an adult when all this happened. She can answer for her own mistakes. I was only a child. I had no influence over what happened to me.

I don't look at my mother [Mary] any differently now than I did before, and the same is true for my adoptive mother. It's just their status has changed. My aunt is no longer my aunt but my birth mother. What I found strangest of all is that their attitude didn't change. I know and they know, but it's obvious that they don't want other people to know. I respected the fact that they didn't want it to affect their lives. My brother knows. My mother has just two sisters, one of whom is my mother. They know and their families know, but nobody on my father's side knows.

I was speaking to my cousin, whose child is adopted, and it was clear that she knows that I'm adopted but doesn't know whose child I am. My mother didn't tell publicly the family, so I don't know who knows, and that is the problem.

I'm not sure if Mary made contact with my father after I was born. I haven't been able to ask. Time is marching on, and one day she will be gone and I will never know. That's what I am afraid of. I wouldn't mind if she said, "I've made a video for you." At least it would be something, but I'd rather sit down with her and talk about it. Not in a hurtful way, because I'm not blaming her for anything, and she knows that at this stage. I don't come across as angry or as a raving lunatic. I'm the same as before and deserve to be told. I'd like her to volunteer the information and to say, "Look, Ian, let's sit down and talk about it. It's not going to be easy, but let's sit down in some neutral venue and talk."

I'm not concerned. It's not a big issue. I'm more intent on making what I'm concerned with right. When the initial questions are answered, then I'd be better able to make a decision as to how to proceed and whether to look for my father, because she might tell me something that I don't know. She might have information that she has been withholding that might be important to me. I don't know anything. I don't know how long she knew him for. I'm not going to feel unwanted if it was a one-night stand. I'd be as nervous as she would be. Life is too short. I just want her to tell me what it was like and to give me the information and leave it at that, and I'd respect whatever she wants. If she would rather people not to know, I'll respect that wish. Once she acknowledges me and the fact that I need to know, then I'll respect whatever she wants, but it does feel unfair to treat it as though it was an everyday occurrence.

A few times I have tried to meet up with my mother so we could sit down together and I could ask her about when she met my father. Did she like him? Did she love him? Was it a one-night stand? Did she see him again? Just all these things you would be naturally curious about. But it has never really materialised. A few times when I attempted to do this, it was a disaster. I think she was very nervous. She had to sneak out of the house. She didn't want her husband to know where she was going, even though he knows I'm her son and I get on very well with him. It's not that he treats her badly or anything, but he seems to use it against her. Or maybe she uses it against herself; I'm really not sure. Anyway, it never worked. One of these occasions was around the time my marriage broke up. She focused more on that as an excuse, saying, "Why didn't it work out?" Deflecting the whole thing. I felt like saying, "Maybe the reason it didn't work is because of what is happening now or what happened in the past — secrecy and everybody hiding things." It wasn't really the cause, but I could have retaliated by using that reason.

Feeling disjointed

From that day to this, I haven't had much more conversation with my mother about it. I've looked at photos and I can see certain physical attributes. I do look like the female side of the Mayberry family. My mother says that I have Mary's traits: my personality, my love of animals, my quiet nature and calmness. My adoptive mother is like the other side of the family, and she can be quite fiery-natured. Mary is very kind and generous. She is easygoing and gently spoken, which is nice.

All I know about my natural father is what I was told by my [adoptive] mother. I know his surname and that he went back to India. I also learnt that he had met me. He saw me once. All this came through my mother when she relayed the original information. I know there is this doctor in Swords who has the same surname. I was saying this to my mother, wondering if he was a relation, and she said, "God, he could be." I was speaking to my natural mother on the phone one night (obviously my mother had mentioned this to her), and she said, "I think that doctor in Swords is his brother." I found it strange that she said this as it's the closest she has ever got to talking about the subject. She was brave enough to say it, or maybe she felt that it took the spotlight off her.

I never pursued that line of enquiry since then, even though the temptation has been there to do so. It would be easy to contact this man and ask. My father would be around seventy-four now. There is a good chance that he is alive. More than likely he has a family who are probably unaware of me. I have a sneaking suspicion that if he is in Ireland he knows about me, because, over the years, I've had a good bit of publicity. He knows the date of birth. If he left Ireland, he just might want to forget about it. But it wouldn't be too hard to go back to Navan (where my father worked) and find out from the records about the details. I don't think there would be a problem with that kind of information.

When you don't know your natural father, you are always wondering where you got certain traits and attitudes from, certain looks and physical characteristics. It's a curiosity at the end of the day.

Teresa

My dream was to be in the Olympics.

A fast-talking, striking young woman, Teresa lives with her hus-
band and two young sons in a large Dublin housing estate. At
the moment, she is completing courses in holistic health and
working as a gym instructor.

She grew up in a family of ten children, all of whom were
adopted. Within the family, Teresa has three brothers who are of
mixed-race parentage, and she maintains close ties with all these
brothers and sisters. Last year, after years of searching, Teresa
made contact with her natural mother. She is still looking for
her natural father, believed to be in Nigeria.

Childhood and growing up

I was taken from St Patrick's Mother and Baby Home when
I was four months old when my adoptive mother took me
to live with her. I never knew that I was any different from
the rest of the children in the house. For years I never knew
that I was black, because when you are a child there are no
problems and you don't see the world for what it is.

My natural mother is a country woman from County
Offaly. She was actually a nun. She told me later that at the
time that she joined the nuns there were no choices but for
a woman to marry as it was unusual to stay single at that
time. Her sister, whom she was close to, had already joined
an order of nuns in Dublin, and my mother followed her
there. She stayed for a year or two but then decided that it
wasn't for her and so she left. She stayed on in Dublin and
worked as a cook in a children's hospital, and there she met
my father, who was Nigerian. At that time, he was studying

medicine at UCD. She says that they were mad about each other and were going out together for about two years; but she does say that they got a lot of hassle as well. She got grief and so did he. At the time it was unusual, and people seeing them together might turn around and say, "What are you doing with that nigger?" She got stared at all the time when she was out with him.

Then she got pregnant, and when she told him he was taken aback. He couldn't believe it at first. He said to her that he had come to Ireland to study and would have to return to Nigeria as a marriage had been arranged for him. But she insists that they loved each other, and she reckoned that, although the circumstances were not ideal, they could have got married and he could have stayed in Dublin, and it wouldn't have really mattered that they were from different cultures. I think that when she found out that she was pregnant, he panicked, and she was very hurt by his reaction to the news. What happened then was that they split up for a while, and then he came back and apologised to her and reassured her that they would sort something out. He paid for her rent in this flat and he bought her clothes and generally looked after her. The only thing was, she says, that they stopped going out together. Then, after a while, time passed and she was forced to leave the flat and move into a mother and baby home.

I was born in March 1967 at St Patrick's Home. My mother says she had a dreadful time. The nuns treated the mothers dreadfully and had them scrubbing and cleaning the place for hours on end. At the time, she was still afraid to go home and tell her parents about the pregnancy. She told her sister, the nun, and her sister advised her to go down home and tell her parents, as she felt that they wouldn't react as badly as my mother anticipated.

My mother was very disappointed with my father for abandoning her. She was very unhappy. It was, she says, the worst time of her life. When I was born, she felt she couldn't give me up for adoption. Even so, the normal thing in the home was for the babies to be adopted, so she went along with this, knowing that the adoption procedure would take a period of time. In the meantime, she heard stories about some of the babies going missing in the night. Some of the mothers changed their minds about adoption, but the nuns insisted that they had to give the babies up. If you weren't married, you really had no choice; the child was taken whether you signed the form or not. Some of the mothers would wake to find their children gone. My mother knew that time was running out, so she asked the nuns would they hold on to me while she went home to tell her parents. It was just a train trip away. Seemingly, they were fine about it, and they told her to bring me down home to them. She went back to get me, but I was gone. The nuns told her that I had been handed over to my [adoptive] mother. My mother protested, saying that she didn't want me adopted and had asked them to hold on to me, but it was too late.

We were all adopted in the family I went to live with. I have six brothers and three sisters. There were actually a couple of stories about us in the paper. One of them had the caption "The most mixed and unusual family", as we were all adopted and some of us were white and some were black.

Back then families tended to be larger anyway, but it was more unusual in that there were four black and six white kids. My three brothers are mixed race, and I found it tough as I was the only girl who was mixed race.

It wasn't a very happy family to grow up in. When I was younger, I didn't know which was worse — growing up being black or being adopted. One was as bad as the other, and the two co-existed inside of me. My [adoptive] mother was very strict. I'm not being unkind, because she did try and do her best. Maybe she took on too much or maybe she took all of us kids to replace that which she didn't have herself, but she took out her resentment on us. When it came to us "black ones", as she called us, she'd say, "I knew I shouldn't have taken you." So your confidence and self-esteem would be very low.

I realised I was adopted when I was four, on my first day at school. I was a different colour and different in that I was adopted, even though I didn't understand the meaning of the word at that time. Like everything else, if you didn't go with the flow you were left aside. I was the only black girl in the school. It was painful to realise that, as, up to then, I felt the same as everybody else. My brothers went to a different school where they had each other for support. Two of my sisters were much older than me and in secondary school by the time I started, so I had nobody — just myself.

I'll never forget what happened on that first day. Nobody would sit beside me. All the other kids were afraid of me. I was happy to go to school and I liked the different activities. Many of the other kids weren't happy to leave their mothers. They were clinging on and frightened, and when they were put sitting next to me they cried even louder. I remember going home that day and telling my older sister that the other kids were calling me names and didn't want to sit beside me. I didn't blame the kids. You could see that they were frightened. If you are different, people sometimes abuse you because of fears they may have themselves. But that first day at school was an awakening for me, and from then on things seemed to go downhill, although I got through it.

I can't actually remember a lot of the things that went on as a child, but I can feel it. At my [adoptive] father's funeral, my older sister reminded me of a particular incident. She was much older than me and at the time she was off to Spain on holidays and told me that she was going to try and get a nice colour like me. Seemingly, I got upset and said, "No, don't do that." I said that if she got a colour like mine, everyone would call her names. She asked me who was calling me names, and I said all the kids called me "blackie" and "nigger" and things like that. My sister was flabbergasted by this and thought it was terrible.

I didn't really understand what adoption was until I was seven years old. My eldest sister used to tell me that it was very special, as most parents had their own children and they got either a girl or a boy and had to be happy with that, whereas I was specially picked out by my mother. So to me it felt like a great thing. When I eventually made friends, they inevitably asked, "How is it that your ma and da are white?" I'd say, "Well, I was adopted," and the first thing that they would say was, "Oh, I'm sorry." And I'd think to myself, *Why are they sorry? What is the big deal?* At that stage, I didn't know what the big deal was, as I still thought I was special. It wasn't a negative thing for me then.

When I got to be a teenager, things looked different. I wished that I hadn't been born, and if I was born, why did I have to be black? Adoption weighed on one shoulder and being black on the other. Being black wasn't something you could hide or something that would allow you to melt into the crowd. It meant being different. I'm not sure how much my upbringing contributed to these feelings that I had at that time. Everyone's pain is different as well. My brothers, who were close in age, were also close to one another. If one of them got picked on, there was another to stand up for him.

My eldest brother did have a rough time though. My mother fostered him before adopting him. Prior to that he was very close to his [former] foster mother, whom he regarded as his real mother, but then she died suddenly.

She had fostered him and a child called Jane, whom he thought of as his sister. When my mother fostered him, she didn't take Jane, who had to go back into a children's home; so they were separated, and that broke his heart. He had lost the person that he though of as his sister as well as his "mother" and had to fit in with this new family with loads of kids. When he did anything wrong, she would ring up the social workers and tell them to take him away, and he'd go back into a home. It was very, very hard for him, and he didn't have to do much for that to happen to him.

Before we hit our teens, we were stood on. We never got the chance to do anything wrong, because for simple things like not putting your shoes in an exact place, we were punished. When I was about ten or so, I reckoned that if I did everything perfectly my mother wouldn't pick on me, but what happened was that she saw me as being too perfect, and she'd say I was doing things just for show. Visitors to the house would say, "Isn't she very good," and my mother would say, "Oh, don't mind her. She's just doing it for show." So you couldn't win no matter what you did.

I was a runner for years and won lots of prizes, but my mother never went to any of these events. My [adoptive] father did go, but I still wanted my mother to be there. I never felt loved by her. Ever. I'd ask my father about things but never my mother, because I was afraid of her. I know at that time parents didn't really talk to their children, but even with personal things, like when I had my first period, I asked my older sister rather than my mother. Strangely enough, the only time she was a bit kind was when you were ill. So, every now and again, I'd pretend to be ill because that was the only time you were pampered.

When I was a child, I know my colour set me apart in many ways. I felt I had to try harder to fit in. In primary school, I was the only black child in an all-white school. By the time I went to secondary school, I was fairly tough. I had built a shell around me that nobody could penetrate. I became what was known back then as a "boot girl", a tough girl. I was very aggressive and afraid to let anyone in. I knew I had to be either tough or weak, as there was no in-between for me. From being slagged in the streets, I knew I had to be strong, so I developed this tough image, but inside I was so soft. If someone blew on me, I'd die. I knew I couldn't afford to be soft as it would be the death of me and I'd end up being one of those kids who was bullied. I made sure that never happened to me. I did stand up for the other girls in the school who were the targets of bullying. I felt I had to help them. In ways, I think my colour helped, as people were a bit intimidated and didn't know what to make of me. As far as the teachers were concerned, I was very unlikeable. I wasn't slow, but I felt it was better to be bold than to be good, because if you were good you got picked on. I was the "messer", but I always tried not to mess to the extent that I was a bully, even though, at times, I did go over the top. Being like that got me through secondary school.

I wasn't very good with people. I kept people at a distance. I'd have one best friend at a time, and I couldn't handle more than one. I couldn't commit myself to more than that. If I was out and about, I'd have lots of mates, but friends were few. I can count on one hand the amount of close friends I've had in my life. Friends would have to get to know me because I'd have left them in, but very few got past the shell I had built around myself.

We all ran away from home at some stage. I ran away when I was twelve, and again when I was fourteen. When I was twelve I stayed overnight at my brother's girlfriend's house. I stayed up telling the girl's mother everything. She told me to stay the night, but my brother found me there. My mother had rung the police because of my age.

My father was a photographer and worked nights. Only for him I'd be dead, I'm sure, as I've been suicidal right through my life, but he kept us together and afloat. My father did stand up for us a lot. He lived in my house for the last year of his life and died a year and a half ago.

When we had all moved away from home and used to go back to visit, we would phone him up when we knew that my mother was out of the house, and five or six used to meet up with him at Dunkin' Donuts every Saturday morning. Once or twice my mother actually passed by on the pavement, and we all ducked down under the table. Now, if I saw my mother walking down the road, I'd cross the road and hope that she hadn't see me. I'd never harm her physically, and even when she is at her worst, I'd still respect her as a mother. At my father's funeral, we all got together and we sat and talked about my mother for the first time as adults and we were all in tears. We spoke to my mother at the funeral so that she wasn't alone, but it was only for that day. Then we walked away.

It was terrible even for my father. That last year of his life, he kept in touch with her all the time. He knew she had nobody, and he used to go down every Friday and give her his pension, and she used to hand him back £5 to live on for the week. When he was living in my house, it was a great year for all of us children. We all got to know him better, and there was none of that hiding in Dunkin' Donuts.

Prior to living with me, my father had moved to live with my sister, and I used to visit him at that time and we got very close. I asked him again to come and stay with me. Finally, one day he arrived up at my house with this small little bag. This is the bag that I carry to college with me every day, and it's like a kind of talisman that makes me feel close to him. In it he had all his worldly possessions. The few clothes he had were from years ago. So I rang her up and I collected the rest of his clothes, and he never went back to live in that house. He stayed with me, and it was the best year of his life for all of us.

Soon after I first met John, I introduced him to my mother. He thought she was wonderful. I had told him certain things about her, but after meeting her, he didn't believe a word of it. One day he came to the house, James [younger brother] had done something trivial. My mother decided to send him to the shop in one of his sister's skirts and a frilly pants. He was fifteen at that time. I thought at first that she was joking, as I didn't believe she would go that far. He didn't want to go, and I was standing there pleading with her not to make him, but she wouldn't listen.

James decided to go to his friend's house a few doors away. His friend's mother opened the door, and I could hear her laughing, as she thought it was some kind of joke until she saw how upset James was. She came across and asked my mother what she was doing. My mother told her to mind her own business.

It was like that with many things, and she seemed quite irrational. I don't hate her. I pity her because she really has nobody now. The youngest two are still living at home. The older of the two works and is in and out of the house quite a bit, but he knows that if things get bad he can come and stay with any of us. My youngest brother is just twelve and he has cerebral palsy, but my mother is older now.

I feel bad in saying these things, as it seems very negative. There were good things, but the bad outweighed them. We were the best-dressed kids on the street, as well as being well fed. We went to Butlin's on holidays, and there my mother relaxed and was a bit less strict. She did show love by buying us things. If she was killing us one day, she would be buying us something the next, and that was her way of showing us love. And she never apologised for anything even when she was in the wrong. She was right and we were wrong, and that was the way it was. Only for my father, I think a lot of us would have had lives that were ten times worse.

Nowadays I try and avoid my mother as I find that the only way to get on with my life, but she dotes on the grandchildren, including my two boys. When they got a little older, they could see the way she treated me, and they asked, "Why does your ma do that?" I could go down to visit her tomorrow and everything could be fine for a few weeks, but then she'd start giving out about my other brothers and sisters, and I wouldn't listen to that. She tries to use one against the other, so I prefer not to let this happen. I talk to the kids about it. I don't hide anything. I feel sorry for them because they don't have a nanny like their mates do. I do visit my mother-in-law, but I feel that, generally, you'd go to your own mother more often and your kids would know your mother better. I've said to the boys that if they want to visit her I wouldn't stop them. I tell them that she is not too bad as a nanny, but I do miss that relationship. I sometimes see mothers and daughters together, and it makes me sad and wish that we could have been like that.

When I was seventeen, I finally packed up and left. Most of my brothers and my two older sisters had left home by the time they reached sixteen or seventeen, if not earlier. I went to England with John, my then boyfriend whom I later married. It was the best time of my life. All that peace. I was in King's Cross for a while and then in Forrest Hill. I had a sister living in Surrey. I felt comfortable. In Ireland, being different was hard. There weren't many black people, but when I went to London, every second person was black. In the beginning, I used to stare in amazement. I felt at home. London was different. The pace of life was much faster, and you wouldn't sit and talk with somebody at the bus stop as you would do here, but as regards race, you wouldn't walk down the road and be called "nigger" because there are so many black people.

During my last few months in London, I felt a bit lonely. I missed people. Plus I missed the rest of the family. There was just John and me, and I didn't know many people. I didn't even know John very well back then. I missed my brothers and sisters, and I also thought if I went back it would be different.

Colour and race

Nobody likes being different. It's like being in a job that pays a wage of £150 per week, and if somebody new comes to the job and they get £151, then World War III breaks out. It's like that with colour. It's like that with everything. Nobody likes difference. You have to be the same.

I actually hate that word "coloured". A lot of black people don't like to be referred to as "coloured". They prefer the term black. Some people, if they are trying to be polite, will use the term "coloured", and people actually find it insulting. I don't get offended when somebody says "that black girl", but I do when somebody says "that nigger" or a term like that.

A lot of the kids who grew up with me would have grown up and settled near where I live, so I know a lot of the faces. Many would probably be the same kids who slagged me when we were growing up. It's really weird because I feel I have got the last laugh. Some of those who used to slag me are dead now. Some are strung out on the corner on drugs. Some are around but they don't seem to be very happy. I walk down the road and see them and I think back to fifteen or twenty years ago. I think some of them do realise that what they did to me all those years ago was wrong and they feel ashamed now. There was one time when one of them came up to me; I didn't remember him, but he recognised me. He said that years ago he used to slag me. He asked me if it was not too late, would I forgive him? He had no idea why he did it. I told him to just forget about it.

I didn't talk to my [mixed-race] brothers about any of this. My brothers are old-fashioned in a way, and they seem to let a lot of things pass over their heads. They don't seem to internalise things, whereas a girl does, and girls talk more from the heart. Men, generally, I think, bottle things up and they don't express their feelings easily. I felt I had it tougher than the lads, although they were older and looked after me. If anybody did anything to me, I could go to my brothers and they would stick up for me. In some ways it was tough for the lads as well, but if they got into a fight, it was more physical and then forgotten. Because I didn't have a sister close in age to me, I grew up close to my brothers, and I tended to be very physical like them, almost like a boy. But we never actually sat down and talked about being coloured. That is why I often wished that I had a sister who was in the same situation as me.

I still get called names to this day. A few week ago, James, my brother who is white, asked me, "Do you get slagged much?" and I said, "Every now and again." He asked me how often, and I said, "Twice, maybe three times a week."

He said that if I had told him that up to a couple of years ago, he wouldn't have believed me. Then he told me about an incident that happened to him the week before. He was with this guy, whom he thought of as his friend. There were two black guys walking down the street. James said he never would have noticed them but his mate said, "All these niggers moving into Ireland."

James said, "What's this 'all these niggers'? We are all the same. It's just different coloured skin." At this stage, this guy didn't know that James had black brothers and a black sister, so he turned to James and said, "Didn't you hear that these people smell like horses?" or words to that effect.

James couldn't believe it. He told him about his brothers and myself, and he warned him never to say anything like that again; and the friend said, "I'm not racist or anything like that, you know." Straightaway he got defensive. James said he knew that things like that happened, but he couldn't really believe it until that incident with somebody whom he thought of as a mate.

When it came to relationships, I think the boys might have had things easier as well. Most of my friends loved my brothers, and they all wanted to have black babies, like it was a fashion of some kind. For me it was a different experience. It wasn't that I didn't look good or that I wasn't a nice person, but boys wouldn't go out with me because I was black, and if they did their friends would slag them. On the other hand, it was thought to be desirable to go out with a black man. This hurt me a lot. Guys that I liked and I knew that they liked me wouldn't take the next step and ask me out because of their mates. And boys who did just did so because black girls were meant to be different and they wanted to see for themselves, I suppose. That was hurtful, too.

There are a lot more black people living here now, particularly in Dublin. In the beginning, I was delighted with this diversity. I used to joke and say it added a bit of colour. But when you overhear conversations, it actually turns out that it hasn't been a positive change. You hear people say, "Those black people all moving into our country, taking our jobs, taking our money." This is really because of the colour of their skin. It's total negativity. I'm still in shock over the reaction people have. I can't believe that it is happening. Recently I was sitting on a bus beside two older women going down Thomas Street. There were a few black women walking past, and immediately they started remarking on "all those coloured people over here". If they were white people, even if they spoke a different language, they would never have noticed. It's all a case of "We don't want them over here."

So it has really made life harder for me, because now people like me are slagged more with "Go back to your own country" and "What are you doing over here?" and stupid remarks like that. When I speak with my thick Dublin accent, people are amazed. A lot of people expect me to speak in some African dialect. It's something that you think you would get used to, but you don't really, and it still hurts. You have to ignore it because you can't fight the whole world, and a lot of people out there are nice, but I do find it worse now. Even when I'm sitting on a bus and there are very few empty seats left, people will hesitate to sit with me. One day on the bus, most seats were taken and I was sitting on the inside seat which was behind the stairwell, so I wasn't immediately visible. The only vacant seat was the one beside me. Somebody got on and came to sit beside me and then looked at me and hesitated and went to stand in the aisle instead. I felt really bad as I know that person didn't sit beside me because he didn't like what he saw. That's hard. It makes me resentful.

I have a brother-in-law, and every time we meet he is always giving out about the refugees. Recently he was giving out that he was seventh on the housing list and is now 400th or something like that because all the refugees have gone ahead of him. It's a load of crap to be honest. He blames everything on the refugees. Sometimes I take it personally, because I feel he is just trying to annoy me. The other day, he said that all the homeless people are on the street and then the refugees coming here and getting houses. I mean, a lot of the homeless people had a home to start with and choose to be where they are. It's completely different, but he doesn't want to understand. Some days it's more bearable than others.

I'm delighted that the refugees have come here because I feel I'm not so easily picked out in a crowd as I would have been before. Of course, as with any group of people, you are going to get good and bad, but I can't believe how quickly Irish people have forgotten the famine and all the people who fled to America during that time and afterwards. These refugees are coming from everywhere, not only black people from African countries, but because the black people are easily identifiable, they are picked out much more easily. Other non-black nationalities may mingle better with the Irish as they don't get as much abuse as the black people. Ireland is a lovely country, and who is to say that you can't move from the UK or America to Ireland if you are willing to work? We emigrate to other countries all the time. And it's not only refugees and asylum seekers coming to Ireland; there are others as well. There shouldn't be a problem, but there is, and a lot of it is caused by ignorance and prejudice. So, if I had to put my hand on my heart, I have to say that Ireland is a very racist country. Someone else might have a different opinion, but you have to be black to see it.

The worst thing that can happen now are my kids getting slagged. The eldest boy, well, you'd never dream that he's coloured. He is blonde-haired and blue-eyed, yet he gets called "blackie" and "nigger" and all that, and he hates it. He used to say to me, "Why do you have to be black, Ma?" That hurts me. The younger boy is like a miniature of me. He has exactly the same colour and eyes. He gets slagged, but he doesn't care. He loves the way he is. He said to me, "Ma, for my confirmation can I have dreadlocks?" and he's really proud of being black, whereas the eldest is ashamed. I feel bad bringing them into the world for that to happen. And I don't want them to be ashamed of me.

Sometimes I ask John if he will take them to school, and he'll ask why, and I'll say, "Jack might be embarrassed." It's OK now because most of Jack's friends know me and know I'm black, but in the beginning they didn't, and he used to ask his dad to collect him rather than me, and I used to get upset. I don't blame him. It's just the reaction of the other children.

I feel sorry for the boys. I try and fight all their wars and I can't. Jack is physically strong, but he won't fight back. If someone hits him and calls him names, he just walks away. The younger one is different. He's not as strong, but if someone calls him a name, he is quite proud to be black and it doesn't bother him. Every time that Jack comes in after being beaten up, I sit him down and talk to him about it. You don't know what to do with kids when this happens. I'm just hoping that it will stop. I've told him that they are doing it to hurt, and if he could pretend to ignore it, they would stop. He says he can't pretend that it doesn't hurt.

I know that a lot of children get bullied. If a child is different in any way, it is bullied. It's as though he can't be different. But what sort of world would it be if everyone was the same? All Jack wants is to be the same as everyone else. I see him going out of his way to be friends with people who bully him, just so that he can fit in with the crowd. He keeps getting hurt, but he goes back for more. It's a real problem, because children carry that with them through life. I'm frightened that it will have a terrible effect on him, because he is very hurt. Really, he is bullied because of me, because he is just a perfect, normal little boy.

Seeking and finding

When I started to think about it, I started to hate my birth parents for leaving me. For a long time I never wanted to meet them as I believed that they had abandoned me and left me in the situation that I found myself in. Even so, I thought about them all the time. I always felt that they would turn up to take me away, but I knew at the same time that it was only a dream and the chance of it happening was very slim.

I thought of my real parents all of the time, but especially at times like birthdays or Mother's Day or Father's Day. More out of curiosity than anything else, I wanted to meet them to see what they were like and to find answers to question like why was I born. I wanted to know about my past.

I didn't start looking while I was still living at home as I was afraid my [adoptive] mother would be hurt, so I thought I would be discreet and wait until I left home. I started looking when I was nineteen. I went to the Eastern Health Board and asked for help. It took me eleven years. They were giving me very little information, and in the end I had to do it myself. First, I went to Barnardos; then I went to the Register of Births. I was going there for weeks and going through files until eventually I found my mother on my own. I was lucky in that she had an unusual second name.

My sister helped, too. She rang up on the pretext of organising a reunion. When she phoned, it was actually my mother's cousin who answered the phone, and she gave my sister my aunt's phone number. My sister phoned that number, and the woman there gave her a number for my mother's other sister, who happened to be the nun that I mentioned earlier. My sister organised for us to go and see her, but, the minute that we got there, this sister said, "This has got nothing to do with a reunion. Has this got anything to do with a child?" My sister admitted that it had and asked how she knew, and she said, "We knew that some day you'd come looking." She phoned my mother and told her that I was looking for her, and from that my mother and myself started corresponding. In the beginning, I checked with my mother whether she wanted me to go through social work channels, but because she had such a bad experience in the past, she didn't want that. We talked on the phone a few times, and last year I met with her.

It was a great relief but a great ordeal at the same time. It was a confusing time for me, and I was all over the place emotionally. I didn't know how I really felt. I was meeting this stranger who gave birth to me that I had no feelings for whatsoever, and I didn't know what way I was going to react. I found out that I had two half-brothers and a half-sister, and I didn't even ask if they knew about me. My main fear going over was my colour, because I always felt if I was white and I went over, there wouldn't be any difficulty, but I worried about what they would think when I turned up — what her kids would think. Would they have negative feelings towards me? There were so many worries. Now I don't know why I worried so much, because when I got there they were all pleased to see me.

When I actually met my mother, we never had very much time on our own. I went with my sister, and we stayed a few miles from where my mother lived. I felt I needed that space. She had wanted me to stay with her, and I think she felt a little hurt that I didn't, but I spent all the time with her. When we got there that evening, I went straight to her house and stayed for three or four hours. The next morning I went back. One of her sons drove a five-hour journey to meet me and brought his little boy, so I met all her family.

Her eldest boy is twenty-nine. I'm thirty-three now, so she got married very soon after leaving Ireland. She only told her sons about me when I made contact with her, but she had told her daughter about me from the time that she was a small child.

On the second day that I was there, we went to the shopping mall, and that was a chance to chat. I had kept saying to my sister, Susan, "Don't leave me on my own," because I was afraid. I didn't know whether to laugh or to cry. After looking for her for so long and finally getting to meet her, it was exciting and frightening at the same time. Susan decided she'd go shopping and give us the opportunity to have time alone. We really only had one hour to ourselves. That is when my mother told me about her relationship with my father. She wanted me to know that it wasn't like a one-night stand, not that it made any difference to me, as I'd have understood. She filled me in a bit on the relationship. I asked her what he was like, and she said that I was very like my father, but she had kept no photos of him. I don't look like my mother physically, but my half-sister and brother have the same eyes as me.

Her kids love the ground that she walks on, and you see them sitting beside her and hugging her quite naturally. They are very close to their mother, and that's why they couldn't believe that she had a child and gave it away. But, as she said to them, "I didn't. When I went back to the home she was gone, and it was taken out of my hands." Her kids seemed really proud of me and even prouder of the fact that I was black, as many of their friends are black.

When I stepped into her house, one of the first things that I saw was a picture I had sent her, a picture of me as a baby, and there it was in a beautiful frame hanging on the wall. She told me, "When anybody asks 'Who is that?' I tell them, 'That's my daughter.'"

She is really proud of me and she doesn't even know me really. She said to me, "I didn't care what way you turned out. I'm proud of you. I just want to apologise for not being there." I told her not to apologise. She feels so guilty, and I feel so sorry for her.

I remember, years ago, my [adoptive] mother said to me that I should look for my parents. I didn't know if she was being cruel or being nice. I asked her why, and she said that she was told that my mother and father had tried hard to get me back but it was too late. It was only years later, when I visited the social worker, that she confirmed that my father had tried to take me. In fact, at the time, the final papers hadn't been signed, but they all colluded against him, as they had done with my mother when I was taken from the home.

My mother told me that two years after I was placed in my adoptive home, she met my father again. She was walking down the street one day and a car pulled up. It was my father, and she said she nearly died when she saw him. She was still very angry with him, and she said to him that she had to give their child away for adoption. He told her he had tried himself to get me back, and she said, "It's too late," and she walked away. Seemingly, when my mother went into a mother and baby home, he had to go back to Nigeria at that time. He told his wife-to-be that he had a child on the way and wanted to try and take me back to Nigeria to raise me as his own and asked her if this would be all right. He must have felt he had sorted all that out, but when he went to the mother and baby home, the nuns wouldn't tell him anything, so he went to the Eastern Health Board. I think the only reason they agreed to see him was because he had qualified in medicine. But at that time there was very little consideration regarding fathers. From knowing that story, I feel that it is possible that he stayed on here or maybe went to work in England, but when I tried to find him, I hit a brick wall. It was actually my father I started out looking for. It's not that I'm not awfully pleased to have found my mother. I think it was more something to do with my feelings about my colour at that time.

So that day, when I was alone with my mother, I asked her a lot about my father. Afterwards I felt bad. I asked myself, *What did I do that for?* I felt, looking back, that I should have talked more about her own life and then, slowly, brought my father into the conversation. I told her that I had been given a name for my father by the Health Board. She told me that she had used a shortened version of his name. My mother says he was about the same age as herself, which would make him about fifty-nine now. She said she was very hurt by the way they split up. She explained to me that it wasn't that she was withholding information, but she just didn't want to talk about him. She said any time she thought about it she felt hurt still as she had loved that man so much. She asked me, if I did find him, not to give him her name or address because she never wanted to see him again. Then I felt that I really shouldn't ask her any more about him.

I think with a mother and child, once you have borne that child for nine months, no matter what colour the child turns out to be, you accept them instinctively. I shouldn't have been afraid of finding my mother, but it's just the way my life has turned out for me, and that's why I was apprehensive. It turned out completely differently to what I had expected. I was thinking, *She's not going to want to see me,* and when she did want to see me, I thought, *She'll only want to see me because she is feeling sorry for me,* but it was quite the opposite. We all got on really well. I'd really love her to come over and meet all the family — my brothers and sisters. They had met Susan, of course, who went with me. My brothers and sisters were all I talked about while I was there. I kept saying, "I can't wait until you meet this one or that one." Then I thought to myself maybe I was talking too much about them, so I had to watch my words, but everything worked out well. When I was leaving, she was upset and crying, and I was crying, too. I call my mother by her first name. I think she would like me to call her "Mum", but I can't. When she used to write to me, she'd sign the letter with her name, and for a long time I'd write something like "Take care, Teresa". I couldn't put "Love, Teresa" because I didn't really know her. We don't speak to each other every day. The last time I spoke with her was about six weeks ago. She'll probably phone me next week, and then it will be another few weeks before we talk again. It's going to take us a long time to build up a bond. It's difficult just talking on the phone.

I felt really sorry for her, and then I felt angry towards him. How could he have left her like that? But later I thought that he probably had to go back home at that time, and these things are unavoidable. The Eastern Health Board said they wrote to his address in Nigeria but there was no response. This was the address which they had from the time that he wrote to the Health Board all those years ago. It was also the address that he had lived at before he started to study medicine at UCD.

In England, when you reach eighteen, it is your right as an adopted person to see the information with the names of your birth parents. You can get in touch with them if they are agreeable. In Ireland, there is nothing like that available, and it is really hard to search.[1]

I had always wanted to go to Nigeria, even on a holiday, to see what it was like because of being half Nigerian. I would love to find him, as I think it would really complete the jigsaw for me. I'm not saying that I'd like him or that we would be bosom pals. It would probably be the same as it is with my mother, because it does take time for a relationship to develop. But it's in my record that he went

---

1 In May 2001 a bill to amend the Irish Adoption Acts was introduced; it relates specifically to the release of information and of original birth certificates to adopted people.

back to the Eastern Health Board on three occasions; I wonder if he has left something for me somewhere — like an address. Did he think then that I would be looking for him all these years later? They weren't very good at keeping information in those days, especially where it concerned men. When you are searching, you come to so many brick walls it's easy to get disheartened.

None of us are getting younger. I would like to find him soon, so I could have a few years of knowing him, like I can with my mother. I didn't tell my mother much about my childhood. She did ask what it was like growing up. I said, "God, I wish you hadn't asked me that."

She said, "So, it was bad?" But I didn't want to tell her everything, and I didn't want her to feel any worse than she already felt.

"My father was brilliant," I said, "but my mother . . . I will tell you about it over time, but I'll just tell you bits at a time."

Now I feel a bit of weight has gone from my shoulders. I feel I'm halfway there, and, as I said, the jigsaw is nearly complete. I'll never feel totally at ease until I find my father. I feel I have to fit those two pieces that were missing together. Before, I always had a slight feeling of being out in the cold. Even if my adoptive parents were the best in the world, I still would have felt the need to look. I think any child who is adopted thinks about where they came from. I think this can take a toll on that person, and it may never leave them.

Effects of childhood

I never heard my [adoptive] mother say the words "I love you". I couldn't even tell you what love is. I've said to my husband, "I do love you," but I don't know how to show it.

He'd say to me, "Teresa, don't be buying me things," because I'd often say to him, "Look what I bought you."

And he'd say "Don't buy me things. Just show me." And I'd say, "How do I show you? I don't know how." I'm only learning now how to show love.

My [adoptive] mother blamed everyone and everything rather than herself. It's like, I'm going to college now. I know I should have done this when I was twenty, and I could say it was her fault that I didn't do it earlier. In some ways it probably was. But at the end of the day, it was more my fault. You can't keep blaming your parents for everything. In a way, I find it hard to differentiate between my colour and the influence of my mother, as one seems to go with the other. I couldn't say that the way I grew up is all associated with my colour as I think some of it has been influenced by my mother. It is hard to pinpoint what has been caused by what.

Sometimes I sit at home and think, "Did that actually happen to me?" Some things are so bizarre that I feel I must have imagined them, and yet I know I haven't.

I don't want to have to deal with a lot of things from my past. I just hope that they go away, but they do come back and threaten me. Some days are good. People can call me anything they want and it wouldn't bother me: I'd still walk tall. Other days, for no apparent reason, someone might stare at me, and immediately I'm on the defensive and would hate being stared at. In the past, I used to dress down so that nobody would stare at me.

Now we are all grown up, you can see how our childhood has affected us. At first I thought our family was the same as most people's families. As brothers and sisters, I think we are closer than a natural family. We had to look out for one another, so it brought us very close, and that is a good thing. Up until a few years ago, I was afraid to go to bed at night because I always had nightmares. I went through prolonged depressions. I've had numerous anxiety attacks, and it stemmed from the way I was brought up. I'm much stronger now, but I feel I only need to be tapped and I'll fall down again. In one respect it has made me strong, but in other ways it has made me kind of cold in that I don't show my feelings. I always tell my kids that I love them a lot, but with people generally I always hold back. I can't show emotions that were never shown to me. On the other hand, I don't attach importance to other people's opinions. In some ways, this is good, but in others it's not. I don't mix very well with people. I keep to myself quite a bit. I'm quite open about talking about my past because I know that all the things that happened to me were not my fault. When I'm feeling bad and things are getting on top of me, I might say something that I'll regret later, but I'll walk away, because I know stuff like that penetrates. It's not something you can wash away. I'd prefer a beating, as I always believed that bruises faded and didn't leave you marked. Saying things like "You'll never be any good" or "You are black and you'll never turn out any good" never really left you.

When I was in my mid-teens, I changed. I started smoking. I started drinking. I ran away. I continued doing that for years, until one day I said to myself, *Teresa, why are you doing this? You are only hurting yourself.* With me it went deeper than adolescent rebellion. I hated my life. I could have ended up on drugs or become alcoholic. My main problem growing up was that I had no confidence. I don't know where I lost my confidence. I don't know if it was to do with my colour or to do with my mother, but anyway I lost it. In the past, I was good at certain things, but I didn't pursue them because of that lack of confidence.

I was a really good athlete. My dream was to be in the Olympics. I won a lot of competitions and championships. Then my mother used to ground me, and when I was grounded I couldn't go to the practice, and because of that I wasn't allowed to enter the competitions. Athletics was my passion. I don't think she realised how good I was. I gave it up because I didn't want her to have that power over me. One of the trainers actually came to the house and said, "Teresa hasn't been training for a few weeks. What's the problem?" and my mother just said, "She's grounded." He asked, "Can you not give her some other punishment?" She wouldn't listen. To my mother, running and athletics meant nothing. I reckon if I had stuck with it I could have been in the Olympics, but I had to give it up. It got to the stage where I couldn't breathe but I was grounded; and I didn't want to tell my trainer, so I gave it up when I was about fourteen.

It was when I gave up running that I started smoking and drinking. I went on a crash diet and was anorexic. That went on for about three years. I went from eight and a half stone to five and a half stone in the space of six months. I did it to see if my mother would notice. My brother who was next to me got worried that I wasn't eating. My mother finally saw what was happening, and, I think, I did get attention from her for a while. She used to supervise my eating and things like that.

I hated being black. I hated living at home. I decided to kill myself. Several times I tried to kill myself, the most recent about six years ago. Up to a few years ago, I drank excessively. Once, I had been very depressed; the doctor gave me pills without trying to look at the root of the problem. One night I took the whole bottle of pills and had a few drinks, and I seriously wanted to die. I thought life was just so hard and being dead would be easier than being alive. It's only in the last few years that I have changed. When the children were young I was occupied, but it is only more recently that I've realised that I have children, and if I did anything silly, they are going to be hurt, and it wouldn't solve all the problems.

At one time, I had separated from my husband for a

while, and I didn't like the way my life was going. Everything was a mess. When I used to go to the doctor with depression, I don't think she realised just how bad I was. That wasn't entirely her fault as I always put on a good face so as not to appear as bad as I was. I never told her that I was suicidal as I didn't want to be taken away in a straitjacket.

So I sat down and talked to myself one day. I decided that I wanted things to be different. First, I decided not to take the tablets any more as they were getting me nowhere. I looked into all kinds of complementary therapies, and then I went to college and studied them. Around that time, I went to relaxation classes in town, and I found it did wonders for me. From then on I changed. I took up holistic studies at college. I think I didn't have time to be depressed in the way that I used to be. I'm not saying that I don't get depressed, because I do, but it's not as bad. Depression, to me, was like losing control over my life. I feel that, over the last couple of years, I've regained that control, and I never want to lose it again.

Depression is very serious. It's one of the biggest killers and leads to things like cancer and heart disease. I always feel that I'm floating in a river and, every so often, I go under. Most of the time I just float along. I don't like going under. It's a horrible feeling. Over the last few years, I've been very good, and I never want to go through that bad depression again. At times, I used to feel that my head was going to explode because I felt so depressed. Then you go to the doctor, and she gives you a few tablets, and you go around in a daze for a few weeks. None of that really helps. Meditation and other things helped me, and that is what got me over it. It's probably different for everybody, but I found Prozac and Valium didn't work for me. I think I could have popped pills for ever and it wouldn't have helped me.

Nowadays I don't go out of my way to make new friends. I like my own company. I don't tend to get involved with things very much. I've been hurt a lot growing up when I went out of my way to make people like me because I was different, but I don't want to do that now. At heart I'm a big softie, but in ways I'm still hurting from the past and still carrying a lot of baggage around with me. You get so sick of telling people the story about being adopted and so on, because the people feel sorry for you, and you just want to fit in. So now I don't give people the chance to hurt me any more. I do my own thing and hope my life is as good as it can be.

Dealing with the past

I think I've gone through all the different stages of anger and bitterness, and now I feel more at peace. I still feel that there is a lot that I would like to be free of. I did go to counselling for a few months, but money wasn't good, and, apart from that, I'm not ready just now. There is a lot of stuff that I still have to face, but the time isn't quite right.

When I was growing up, I hated being black. I knew there was nothing I could do to change it. For a while I hated the white part of me because white people slagged me. Even though I was half white, they only saw the black part. Then I went through another phase where I didn't feel that I was accepted by black people either. I'm not black and I'm not white, and it got to the stage where I hated both. Now I'm happy the way I am. I'm happy that I'm black and white as I reckon I have the best of both worlds. If black people don't accept me, that's fine. And if white people don't accept me, that's fine, too. The way I look at it, I am who I am, and if you don't like me — that's tough.

There are a lot of things that I'm not completely happy with. I had to become a certain type of person to survive.

It's only now that I'm starting to be myself and to live life in a different way than before. I can honestly say that the best thing that has happened is being black and adopted, as these things have made me very strong. Otherwise, it has been a very sad life for me as well, but I suppose it cuts both ways. It makes you very strong, as you have to work harder to get places. You fall down, but you jump back up again. I'm starting to do things now that I should have done in my twenties. I ask myself why I didn't do these things back then, but I needed to sort myself out first. Now I find everything is starting to work for me. I'm a bit frightened as well, and I'm waiting for things to go wrong, but I shouldn't think like that as I'm trying to be positive. I'm doing really well at college. I'm a qualified therapist in massage, reflexology, physiology and stress therapy. I'm working as a gym instructor teaching aerobics, so I'm doing work that I really love. If anybody had said to me five years ago that I'd be a therapist, I would have laughed. I thought I'd never be anything. To go in and take a class now gives me a fantastic feeling and I love it. I needed something of my own apart from my marriage and the kids. I'm very pleased and still a bit incredulous that I'm paid to do something that I love so much.

Colour sometimes has advantages. Companies at times have to employ somebody with a form of handicap or disability as they can't discriminate, and occasionally I have sometimes benefited from that.

When one parent is black and one is white, the child is in-between. I've sometimes been called a mongrel. I always say that I got the best of both worlds, but I wonder, if I ever meet my father, how it would be for me. In Nigeria, I wouldn't be considered black, but here I am; so where do you stand? When my father went back to Nigeria, I wonder how my life would have been if he succeeded in taking me with him. Nigerian culture is very different. I read a bit about it, and, in many ways, I'm glad I wasn't reared there because women seem to take second place to men. Maybe if I was brought up in that way, I wouldn't know any differently, but I'm glad I was brought up in Ireland. Even though I'm not completely happy about my upbringing, I've had the chance to have my own voice.

I still have a bit of pain, but I hope that this can be sorted out. I don't think anything can touch me now. I feel really strong, and I feel that I am really going places. My confidence is lifted. I don't hurt as much. If someone calls me a name, it still hurts, but not as much as in the past. And I am happy now with the way I am — a bit of both. I'm happy I'm not white and I'm happy I'm not black. Life is starting to work out for me, and I have come through it all.

Curtis

A black Irishman, that's me . . . Nobody can take that away from me.

Thirty-one-year-old Curtis Fleming has spent more than a decade playing professional football with Middlesborough Football Club.

Despite his protestations of not being organised or ambitious, he is a shining example of all that is best about sport, with his passion for the game and a deep loyalty to his old clubs and mentors as well as to his present club.

Apart from this love of football, he is devoted to his family and to his late mother, who died when Curtis was nineteen and whom he continues to miss greatly.

Early life

I was born in Manchester, but my mum brought me back to Dublin when I was six months old. There were a lot of arguments going on between her and my dad. I don't think he was into Ireland at all, so she came back on her own with me. She had lived in Manchester for a few years, and after a while she went back to my dad and ended up down in London. My brother was born there and my sister was born in Dublin when Mum moved back here for good.

It's only Ballybough that I remember. You could put me in the middle of Manchester and I wouldn't have a clue where I was. I class Ballybough and Dublin as my home. I'm so proud of these Irish roots. It says on my birth cert that I was born in Manchester, but it doesn't mean a thing to me.

My mum was originally from the Ballybough flats, and later her mother moved to one of those houses off Clonliffe Road, and that's where we all grew up. There were a lot of

217

people in the house — my granny and five or six uncles and aunties and then us. The others all moved on to houses of their own. We ended up in the family home, and we had loads of relatives all around. My mum's mum had been married twice, so there was a double family, the Duffs and the Flemings. Loads of uncles and aunts, and they were all brilliant to us when we were small. Most of them still live in Dublin. One uncle lives about an hour and a half's drive away from me in England, and I go down to see him often. He has two sons who were born and bred over there, but he makes sure that they know about Dublin. He follows Celtic and is very into Irish music, as that side of the family are very musical.

My mother's parents died before I reached my teens, and she ended up bringing up the rest of the family. She was a middle child. Some of my uncles were older than her, but she was the eldest girl, and it seems she took over. She was a strong-willed kind of woman. All my uncles really adored her because they felt the family would have fallen apart at the time but for her. She had a hard life; and then she brought us up on her own and died when she was only forty-two, so it was terrible really.

Strangely enough, my mum's mother also died aged forty-two, also of cancer. It's a waste of a life, but when you are eighteen, forty-two seems old. Now I am thirty-one, it's very young. So I didn't really know my granny. Yet she comes across as a strong woman as well because she brought up all those kids on her own.

I've got two kids. One is four and the other is two and a half, and they are brilliant. They are close in age so they are friends as well. I do OK financially and can look after them. I don't mean for ever, but they have a secure childhood. We don't have to worry too much about bills, but in other ways we sometimes find it difficult enough, so I wonder how my mum coped with the three of us by herself. It's amazing.

Childhood experiences and starting with football
I went to St Mary's Primary School and then on to St Joseph's Christian Brothers' School in Fairview, which was just ten minutes away. I enjoyed school. Myself and my brother were the only two coloured kids in the school. I think when you are that age, the younger kids are inclined to abuse you about your colour, and it can upset you very deeply. I remember the stick I got about my colour at primary school, but less so when I moved to secondary. My brother was two years younger and he was taller than me, so it was fine in that we always stuck together and had support if one of us got into scrapes or anything like that. He was bigger than me and a bit more outgoing and a bit more aggressive, so the two of us looked out for one another in primary school. We were probably closer then than we have ever been since.

I remember once when we got into trouble at school: it was a black thing. A boy called me a "kaffir", which is a term that comes from South Africa. My mum was quite politicised, so we'd know about events in South Africa and union things. Other kids wouldn't have known these things. We did because we were brought up with it, so I understood exactly what he was saying when he called me a kaffir. He called me a "black bastard" as well, so I got into a fight and went home with my jumper all ripped.

My mum just said, "You better understand that you are black, Curtis. You are not a bastard but you are black, and those boys are just uneducated if they make statements like that."

My mum was brilliant, I thought. She brought us up fantastically well so that we were able to handle what came along. She explained that they were just ignorant, and at the end of the day, we had a different colour but we were the same as her, the same as everybody else. She made us proud of who we were. Sometimes it did get to you and you just couldn't handle it, but more often than not there were no problems.

I think small kids can be more hurtful. You get all that "nig nog" and those other silly names that you are called, so from an early age the difference is pointed out to you by the other kids. I remember another incident in primary school when me and my brother got surrounded by a load of boys from the Ballybough flats. They were all around us in a circle, calling us "nig nog" and things like that. It was very upsetting. It must have been, because I can still remember it now. It was probably one of the most hurtful things that ever happened to us. I mean, people would have called me names as the years went on, but I was able to handle it. Those same boys could probably never understand our pain or even remember that day, but it is still alive in my mind, even now.

I made sure it didn't happen again. It was about to start again when we were in secondary school. One of the boys who was part of the group from primary school tried the same thing, and we battered him, and that was it. That helped me in a way, because you could see that people were thinking, *You don't mess with him.* It was an incident that had a big influence on me, because afterwards I was thinking, *I'm not going to be surrounded by a group of boys chanting, with my brother crying all the way home.* It's a horrible, horrible feeling.

Later on, when you are fifteen or sixteen and going out with somebody, you might be nervous about going to some girl's home. The father is standing there, and you can see him thinking, *What's this black guy coming to my home for?* You have to deal with those feelings, too.

I think, if we didn't have a parent who was as strong as my mum, they might be more inclined to say, "Well, keep out of the way. Keep away from them." But if you go hiding in the schoolyard, those bullies will smell your fear. I can't remember the exact advice my mum gave when we came home from school crying, but it must have been good, because I can't remember it happening much after that. She would have said, "That's the colour you are," and we felt accepted. I think it was a little easier for my sister. My sister is a lot paler. She got stick as well, but her school was right beside ours, and she always had her two big brothers. I think that helped her a bit. On the other hand, if she had problems she might not always have told us as she would know that we would get involved.

People tend to think that all black guys are athletic, but so many have no interest at all in sport. My brother would have a better physique, but he's not really into sport. They do tend to stereotype black guys as being strong and athletic, but it is all very individual. We are influenced by how we were brought up by our mum. We went to acting classes as kids, so if I had a leaning towards acting, maybe I'd have been drawn to that, but it wasn't for me. I found what I wanted to do in football.

A football career

I was playing football from when I was seven. My brother started playing at about the same age, but he was involved in a lot of other things at the same time, whereas I was just into football and was very focused on playing. I really loved it and played all the time. When I go back to the street where I grew up, all the neighbours say to me, "You were a nightmare," kicking a ball all the time. My mother had to drag me in off the street.

I played schoolboy football at Belvedere when Noel [O'Reilly][1] was coaching us, and Brian [Kerr][2] did a bit as

---

1   Assistant coach with the Irish Junior International Soccer Squad.
2   Coach with the Irish Junior International Soccer Squad.

well. I joined when I was eight and left when I was eighteen, which was a long time. I was very happy there. It was based in Fairview, near my school and near my home. The manager, who is now a good friend of mine, remained the same throughout all the time that I was there. My brother went to play for them as well. It was a great club, and they looked after us like a family. When I look back now, there was a lot of stability in my life through all that time.

By the time my mum died, I was playing with St Patrick's Athletic. I had a lot of support there as well. Brian Kerr was brilliant with me if I had any problems in the home or anything. Looking back, I can see that my brother and sister didn't have that type of support that I did, but when you are eighteen you don't realise these things. You are not trained to look after younger kids. Nobody tells you what to do.

I didn't go over to play football in England until I was twenty-one. I was playing with St Pat's and worked in a clothes shop near Stephen's Green, so I went to England when I was quite old. Everyone says you should go when you are sixteen. I had plenty of trials, but I wasn't dedicated enough at the time. I think at that age I was too relaxed, but then how serious should you be at sixteen? But I really believed that at some stage I would go to play in England. I have the same conviction now that, when I finish my professional career, I'll be OK. I have a lot of good friends, and something will work out for me.

The only thing about football is that, in a way, it masks your colour. People look at me and say, "He is Curtis, the footballer," rather than saying, "There is Curtis, the black guy." But, when you find yourself in unfamiliar places, you see other reactions, and you realise how racist people can be. You hear comments that you mightn't otherwise hear. So, to a certain extent, football can cushion you from racism.

Mother and father

My father is from Kingston, Jamaica. He moved to England with his brother and they settled in Manchester, but they also moved around a bit. When I was a kid, I didn't see much of him. I know where he lives and I have spoken to a half-sister, but I really have no inclination to go and meet him. There is no connection there. My mum brought us up, and she did a brilliant job at a difficult time, and that's good enough for me.

One reason why I am not very interested in meeting my dad is because I think the strongest and bravest person I have ever met is my mum, bringing up black kids in Dublin in the late sixties. Over the years things have got better, but I can imagine what it was like back then. I can remember my mum mentioning about some neighbours staring and whispering. It must have been so difficult for her.

She was an actress, and she was in work and out of work. I think we had a very good childhood, and I think she was the bravest of women. All of my uncles are musicians. I'm especially close to all my uncles as my mum was like a mother to them. Many of them are involved in the unions. A few play with a traditional band. My mum sang as well as acting. She did different workshops and acted in the Abbey and the Gaiety. She travelled in England, and she went to Berlin with the Connolly Youth Movement. I remember her showing us the photos of her time in Berlin. But I think my greatest memory of her was of her music. There was always music in our house. I laugh now because I listen to Nina Simone and John Denver, and people say to me, "How do you listen to that?" and I say, "I heard it at home every day." I think music was one of the biggest gifts that our mum gave us. Then she would be practising her lines, and I would stand in and listen to her lines. I think it was an unusual kind of childhood. Later on, I think it gave me a much broader outlook on life that I wouldn't have had if I had grown up in an ordinary house with a mum and dad on an ordinary street. We used to have different actors coming back to our house after shows, and we went to concerts and to plays and to see my mum performing.

I don't know much about my father. At the end of the day, my closeness to my mum meant that I had no desire to be close to him. My mum did talk about him when I was younger, and my brother and sister went to stay with him in England for about a month. He asked me if I wanted to go, but I refused. I knew my mum would miss us if we all left for a whole month, but she was happy that they visited him. Before she died, she told me that what happened between them was a case of two people falling out and agreeing to separate. She said that it wasn't that my dad left her but that they decided to live separately. She said, "You should try not to hate him." But my thoughts were, and still are, that she was left on her own bringing up these three coloured kids in Dublin all that time. Maybe if I spoke to him now he would be able to explain the reasons why they split up, which would be more interesting to me now that I am older. We will see. Maybe some day. But probably not in the near future.

You could win the lottery tomorrow, but you can't bring her back. It puts a different perspective on everything. When I think about it, it was probably very hard for my brother and sister when she died. I think ever since then they have struggled a bit, whereas I kept going with football and other things, but I don't think you ever feel the same again. I always feel that something is missing. I wasn't exactly the apple of her eye, but I was always there. She went through a lot of things with me. When I was two, she had my younger brother. He was still a baby when I was three years old, and she always said that I kept her spirits up, smiling and things like that. So as I was growing up I grew very close to her, but she adored the three of us. I don't know how she did it, because we always had the best football boots and went on the school trips and things like that. She did brilliantly.

Racism, football and anti-racism
I'm involved in the campaign in England "Kick Racism out of Soccer". I go to meetings sometimes where I get talking to people in ordinary nine-to-five jobs, and I'll meet someone who will say, "I get stick at this and that." In some ways, in football you are shielded from that, but, on the pitch, you definitely get it. I think it was much worse a few years ago, especially with the terracing. They have made stadiums all-seater now, and all the loudmouths can't congregate together.

With the terracing in stadiums, up to a few years ago, you would get a group of maybe a hundred guys together, and if one started shouting racist slogans and making the monkey noises, they would all join in. It's horrible and it does get to you at times, but the more it happens, the more you learn how to deal with it. It happens in League of Ireland games as well, particularly when we'd go to away games. Playing in front to two or three thousand people, you can actually hear individual comments, and it's not nice. It can get you down. If you are playing in front of forty thousand, you can't hear these individuals because it's such a block of people.

Thinking back to when I was in school, football kept me going. In school if you were a good footballer or a good GAA player or a good hurler, it didn't matter what colour you were. You were in the school team, scoring goals, and it was a case of "Are you all right, Curt?" and colour goes out the window. I played for Ireland when I was seventeen. From the time I was fifteen, I played for Dublin and for Leinster. At the end of the day, everyone knows you as a good player or knows about you. It gives you a type of confidence to an extent that you don't need to hide in a corner.

This is my tenth year in Middlesborough. It's my first and only club. I'm content there and I appreciate what I get. I probably could have done better in my ten years in England if I moved clubs, but I'm settled and I'm happy with the club. Before that, and after my mum died, I think I didn't feel settled. You tend to worry, and I wanted a base more than moving all around the place: to have a base, a nice house and to have no problems. I think stability is important, especially when you have kids. If you are moving all around the place, you can't be sure what effect it has on the kids, and they are your number one priority. Until you have a child, you don't really realise how important it is to make sure that they are OK.

I did a bit of work with Frank [Buckley][3] and with the campaign "Show Racism the Red Card" in England. In fact tomorrow,[4] the Irish squad are being photographed holding red cards. This is organised by the English campaign. They have done brilliantly and have the support of some of the top players and managers in England, high profile players like Dennis Bergkamp and Thierry Henry. These guys are the top players in the world, and when you have support from them, you know you are on the right track. I helped Frank, and I went to last year's SARI, to a five-a-side game in the grounds of the Law Society in Blackhall Place. I did a bit as well for "Football Mondial", which was a programme on Sky. We also did a few interviews and a press conference in the Sports Café in Temple Bar. I don't really like speaking to the media, but that was OK.

---

3 Organiser of Sport Against Racism in Ireland (SARI).
4 Wednesday, 11 October 2000, at the World Cup qualifier between Republic of Ireland and Estonia at Lansdowne Road.

I didn't understand how bad it was for travellers until I was playing with St Pat's. We played in a five-a-side competition in Finglas, and they had a travellers' team in the competition. We won, and everyone went back to the pub for a drink, and the travellers were asked to leave. So, that being the case, we said we would all leave, and the lads said it was like that everywhere they went. They were banned from most pubs. I'd never known that. Then again, I'd never known any travellers, and the only travellers I ever met were the ones who knocked on the door selling carpets.

In football administration, you get people who have been a long time in office and are not aware of the changes that are taking place. They are not involved at grass-roots levels and can be out of touch. I spoke to Noel and Brian, and they told me that here in Dublin there is a Croatian team and a team from the Congo in the league and a Romanian team as well. I don't think this is an initiative from the FAI. I think you need a new breed of people, like Noel and Brian, people who know exactly what is going on at the grass-roots. You can have ideas and initiatives for this and that, but if you leave it to the bureaucrats it's going to be a case of "We will bring it up at the next meeting," and it's less likely to happen.

I find sport hugely positive. We all have a love for the one thing and spend so much time doing it and talking about it that it brings you closer. When we socialise and go out for a pint, we end up talking about football. On a night out, you could sit for four or five hours talking about football, but you know that the others aren't going to be bored. They won't be thinking, "There he is, off again," because we all have the same interest. All aiming for the same thing and all wanting to do well. All with the same goal of winning a league or avoiding relegation, and you can't do it yourself. You have to pull together.

Irish roots

We had a stable family life. On the occasions when my mum was on tour, we might just go and stay with an uncle. With my mum, her house was her castle. We didn't have a lot in it, it wasn't furnished fantastically well, but it was home, and it was brilliant for us. We were happy there, and that house was very important to her.

The house is still there. My sister lives there now, and my brother comes and goes. They have their own lives. I find it hard when I go home because I think you need a mum to be there, to keep you together, because you all end up just splitting. It's a mum that keeps you going, seeing that you come together on a Sunday for dinner. We don't have that any more and tend to go our separate ways. Your mother and the love that you have for her is what you have in common. Now she is gone, you can see how we all have separate lives. There is nobody there to say, "I want you all here on Sunday" or "Don't fall out with him." It's terrible really. It has been a huge change for all of us.

It would be so good if she was still around now. For one thing, you would get the whole story, because I was eighteen going on nineteen when she died and I didn't question things as much at that age. At that time, I was more involved in clubbing and going into town. I had a very different outlook to what I would have now, especially having kids of my own.

I think the thing that helped me out a lot was my Dublin accent. When I was younger and out with my mates, I would see people looking at me strangely. I'd be standing beside them and I'd feel them looking; then I might say something like, "Any chance of a pint?" They would look in amazement and say, "Where are you from?" and when I'd say, "Ballybough", they'd immediately notice the accent and that was the end of it.

I went to Glasgow a few weeks ago with my wife to meet

some friends. We went to an Indian restaurant, and all the Indian guys there had Glaswegian accents. I thought it hilarious and was laughing, and my wife said, "What are you laughing at?" They were probably looking at me and thinking, "He has an Irish accent." She said, "They are probably all laughing at you, Curt." But in Dublin the accent really does help. I have been away ten years. I think, maybe in the first year, you develop a little twang in your voice, but after that, I think, you become more Irish when you are away from home. You become more proud of your roots and your traditions. I speak a lot deeper when I'm in Dublin. When I'm away, I speak in a milder tone. The reason for that is because I wouldn't be understood otherwise. Sometimes I'll come back from Dublin and the lads will say, "Been away have we?" because I'm rabbiting away, but then I'll change back to my milder accent. You just switch on and switch off and it's quite unconscious, but I don't think I've ever lost it or ever had any English tone in my voice.

When I was growing up, my mates were mainly people I met through football. Many of them were from around Thomas Street and Oliver Bond, so I ended up on that side of the city quite a bit. Then when I was sixteen, I was going clubbing, so I was around town all the time. If you asked anyone of my age where they went to socialise, you'd find that we all went to the same places. None of my mates would stand for any form of racism when I would be out with them. Sometimes I'd say, "Ah, leave it," but they'd say, "No", and it would go further with them.

The only time that I got into trouble, and it happened a few times, was when lads thought I wasn't from Ballybough. They assumed I was English and wanted to fight with me, but then they would hear me speak, and everything would change. My mates would come over to them and say, "What do you think you are doing?" That would happen simply because I was mistaken for being English. I was never seen as being from Africa or from America. It's quite funny, and I'm not sure why that was, but it was probably because you would never really see African or Jamaican guys around Dublin at that time. It would usually be English guys who had come for a weekend trip because it is only a short ferry ride away.

At the SARI day in Dublin last year, I met guys from the Congo and Zaire. It was amazing to see all these different nationalities here in Ireland. This is probably the reason why a lot of people are afraid just now. People tend to be afraid of things that they can't understand. If somebody says, "There are a load of them coming into the country," then people will believe that. It is like the Irish going to England years ago and being greeted by those signs saying "No Irish or blacks". I was watching a programme recently about how important Irish immigrant labour was to the workforce in England in building the motorways and other things. They couldn't have done it at the time without the Irish labourers, and yet all of that time you had those notices displayed everywhere. It's amazing to think that this was only forty years ago.

Racism is a problem in Ireland at the moment. Maybe every country has to go through it. In England it happened years ago, but in this country we have to go through it now. When I first got abused as a footballer, I used to get upset. Then I thought about it and I felt, *They are idiots. Why are they paying money to go to watch a game just to abuse somebody?* It is very stupid when you think about it.

Being in England makes me feel more Irish. At the end of the day, I'm a black Irishman. I'm proud of my roots. I'm proud of being from Dublin, and I'm proud of my mum and being brought up as Irish. The lads give me a bit of stick at times when I'm in England. They say, "Well, where were you born?"

I say, "I was here [in England] for four months. If that makes me English, fair enough, but I've spent twenty-one years in Ireland. I'm Irish. My passport is Irish and my whole identity is of Ireland."

I class myself as coloured or black or mixed race. In the north-east of England where I live, there are not as many ethnic groups as you would find in places like Leeds or Manchester or London. In London there is an unbelievable variety of people. You find whole areas of black or Chinese or Asian people. In the north-east, you do get a number of Asian people who have set up businesses. In Ireland, there is much more variety of people, and this has all happened quite suddenly. I don't mind which of those words are used to describe me. They are fine by me. But in England, I might have a problem if I use the term "black". In England, the black guys are really black, and they would call me "coloured". In their estimation, I'm not a real black man, but a white guy would class us all as being the same.

I have a very strong sense of identity. A black Irishman, that's me, and I'm proud of it. Nobody can take that away from me. I think once you are happy with what you are, people come to accept you. I've never been ashamed of being Irish or being black, but, I think, when you are five years old and getting hassle about it all the time, you'd probably be thinking, *I wish I wasn't black*. But then kids who are overweight and who get hassle probably feel the same. As you get older, you understand better who you are, and you don't see why you should change. I mean, I'm not going to be a white Irishman suddenly. I was born black and Irish and I'll die that way. You have to enjoy and appreciate who you are. This happens more easily as you mature.

Looking forward, looking back

Both of my children are very sallow. They look white, but they can't get away from colour because of their dad; and they can't get away from Ireland or that heritage. They have been in Dublin several times. I try and bring them almost every time I come home. I think it's very good for them to experience a different culture from this early age, and I think that it's great for them. If I do meet up with my dad, then they will know that he is Jamaican; and that is another culture and another part of the world that they can visit. With colour, I'm not sure if they will look darker when they are older, but there is nothing you can do about it. Any questions or any problems they may have, then they can ask me, as I have been through it already.

I come back to Dublin three or four times a year when I get the chance. I have a lot of good friends here that I catch up with. It depends on how much time I have, but when I'm on international duty with the Irish soccer squad, it usually gives me extra time back here. I keep an eye on all my friends. A lot of people are inclined to lose touch with their real friends when they go away to play professional football in England, but I know that at the stage when I've packed in professional football, I can come back and my friends will still be there. I can sit and have a cup of coffee with Noel now like I would have had ten years ago, and I could still have a cup of coffee with him in ten years' time. I hope my friends feel the same about me, because I believe that you shouldn't change. I think you develop in different ways as you go through life experiences, and, especially when you have kids of your own, your priorities change, but for me there is a lot of continuity with the past when it comes to friends. One of my best mates is somebody I played football with when I was sixteen. Most of my friends are from playing football. I've seen some of my mates do so well, and I'm so proud of them.

I suffered from homesickness a bit when I went to England first, but probably not as much as some of the younger ones did. By the time I went away, I had worked in shops and in security jobs. I was used to being on my feet at work for eight or nine hours a day and I understood what work was about. When I went to Middlesborough, I appreciated it a lot more than some of the lads who were younger than me and who had come straight from school. I thought it was great to be doing what I liked best and to be earning good money to do it. To me it was brilliant, but, at the same time, I have no fears about going back to work. My contract with Middlesborough is up this year, so we will have to see what happens. My wife will stay where we are with the kids, and I might commute if I was to move to another club. We are settled where we are and the kids are happy, but, if needs be, we could move because it is a short career. We will just wait and see what happens.

Another Irish trait of mine that is probably annoying for other people is being very laid-back and relaxed. My wife and my mates ask, "What will you do?"

I always say, "It will be all right. Something will happen. I'll be grand." Something will happen. I know it will. I'm not quite sure what I want to do, maybe a bit of business. I'm not sure if I would like to be involved in business, but it is just to get a taste of it and see. I could go into coaching. I could do agency work, bringing Irish kids over to England. There is something out there for me. Something will happen.

Further Reading

Brown, Y., and Montague, A. *The Colour of Love: Mixed Race Relationships.* London: Virago, 1991.

Bryon, B.; Dadzie, G.; and Scafe, S. *The Heart of the Race: Black Women's Lives in Britain.* London: Virago, 1985.

Bugis, G. ed. *Migrant Women Crossing Borders and Changing Identity.* Oxford: Berg Publications, 1993.

Cullen, P. *Refugees and Asylum Seekers in Ireland.* Cork: Cork University Press, 2000.

Fitzgerald, G. *Repulsing Racism.* Dublin: Attic Press, 1992.

Funderberg, L. *Black, White, Other.* New York: William Morrow, 1994.

Gannon, F. "The Vietnamese in Ireland: Grieving on Two Shores", Masters thesis, University of Dublin, Trinity College, 1996.

Hart, W. "Blue Men and Black Men: The Presence of Africans in Ireland 1550–1950". Unpublished paper delivered at a meeting of the African Cultural Project, Dublin, September 1995.

Kay, J. *The Adoption Papers.* Newcastle Upon Tyne: Bloodaxe, 1998.

Knight, S. ed. *Where the Grass is Greener.* Dublin: Oak Tree Press, 2001.

MacGreil, M. *Prejudice in Ireland Re-visited.* Maynooth: Survey and Research Unit, Department of Social Studies, 1996.

MacLachalan, M., and O'Connell, M. *Cultivating Pluralism: Psychological, Social and Cultural Perspectives on a Changing Ireland.* Dublin: Oak Tree Press, 2000.

Maslow, A. H. *Towards a Psychology of Being*. New York: Van Nostrand, 1962.

Tannam, M.; Smith, S.; and Flood, S. *Anti-Racism: An Irish Perspective*. Dublin: Harmony, 1998.

Tannam, M. *Racism in Ireland: Sources of Information*. Dublin: Harmony, 1991.

Tizard, B., and Phoenix, A. *Black, White or Mixed Race?* London: Routledge, 1993.

SOME OTHER READING
from
BRANDON

Sean O'Callaghan

To Hell or Barbados
The Ethnic Cleansing of Ireland

The previously untold story of over 50,000 Irish men, women and children who were transported to Barbados and Virginia.

"An illuminating insight into a neglected episode in Irish history, but its significance is much broader than that. Its main achievement is to situate the story of colonialism in Ireland in the much larger context of worldwide European imperialism. O'Callaghan's description of seventeenth century Barbados is a powerful portrait of a society as brutal, corrupt and unjust as anything the twentieth century has to offer. Yet it is precisely societies like colonial Barbados and Virginia which lie at the root of our modern world. That is why *To Hell or Barbados* is such a valuable book." *Irish World*

ISBN 0 86322 287 0; 256 pages; Paperback

Bernard O'Mahoney
with Mick McGovern
Soldier of the Queen

"Forget those SAS memoirs. Ex-soldier Bernard O'Mahoney knows what life was really like fighting an everyday war against the IRA." *Maxim*

"Captures perfectly the life of a British soldier at a key point in the history of Ireland in the late 20th century, and it is acidly funny. . . [It] is as good a book as you are likely to find about military life and soldiering in Northern Ireland." *The Irish Times*

ISBN 0 86322 278 1; 256 pages; Paperback

www.brandonbooks.com

Alison O'Connor

A Message from Heaven
The Life and Crimes of Father Sean Fortune

"Explosive. . . well-researched and tightly written."
The Irish Times

"Compelling. . . Its meticulous presentation of the evidence leaves no doubt as to Fortune's appalling catalogue of crimes against children." *Sunday Tribune*

"Gripping and compulsive." *Sunday Business Post*

"Highly readable. . . devastating in its cool clarity and detail." *Irish Independent*

"Forthright, unsensational." *Enniscorthy Echo*

ISBN 0 86322 270 6; 256 pages; Paperback

Gerry Adams
An Irish Journal

A unique insight into recent Irish politics, this new book covers the crucial period between mid-1997 and the end of 2000. Consisting in the most part of selected articles from his regular column in the New York newspaper, *The Irish Voice*, these writings provide not only a revealing chronicle of the peace process but also an insight into his private life, and some surprisingly light and humorous moments.

ISBN 0 86322 282 X; 288 pages; Paperback

STEVE MACDONOGH
Open Book: One Publisher's War

"MacDonogh is without doubt the most adventurous and determined of the Irish publishers . . . This is an important book." *Phoenix*

"An intelligent, informative account of a life spent fighting for freedom of speech, a right which is still not adequately safeguarded." *Irish World*

"A fascinating and very important book." Brid Rosney, Today FM

ISBN 0 86322 263 3; 256 pages; Paperback

EAMONN MCCANN
Bloody Sunday in Derry
What Really Happened

A new edition of the classic account of Bloody Sunday. "A highly successful formula of 'unsanitised' primary sources, oral history and political commentary and analysis. The layout of the book makes for easy reading of a complex and disturbing truth." *Books Ireland*

"This moving and impressive book is cumulatively powerful. The *tour de force* of the book is its description of Lord Widgery's Tribunal." *Guardian*

ISBN 0 86322 274 9; 256 pages; Paperback